Songs of the Tewa

Translated by
Herbert Joseph Spinden

Preface by Alice Marriott

SUNSTONE
PRESS

Library of Congress Cataloging-in-Publication Data:
Songs of the Tewa / translated by Herbert Joseph Spinden: preface by
Alice Marriott.—2nd ed.
    p.   cm.
English and Tewa.
"Originally published under the auspices of the Exposition of Indian Tribal
Arts, Inc. in 1933"—T.p.verso.
ISBN 0-86534-193-1 : $12.95
   1. Indian poetry—History and critism. 2. Tewa poetry—Translations into English.
I. Spinden, Herbert Joseph, 1879-1967.
PM167.S58   1993   92-33989
897—dc20   CIP

Published by   Sunstone Press
                 Post Office Box 2321
                 Santa Fe, New Mexico 98704-2321 / USA

Photographs from the collection of Mrs. H.J.Spinden and the Photo Archives of the Museum of New Mexico. This book originally published under the auspices of The Exposition of Indian Tribal Arts, Inc. in 1933.

TABLE OF CONTENTS

AUTHOR'S PREFACE

THIS LITTLE BOOK VOICES AN APPRECIATION OF THE ETHICS AND IDEALS OF THE AMERICAN INDIAN AS THESE ARE EXPRESSED IN HIS MOST ENDURING WORDS. I AM INDEBTED FOR ITS PUBLICATION AT THIS TIME TO THE EXPOSITION OF INDIAN TRIBAL ARTS INC., AN ORGANIZATION EFFECTED IN 1930 FOR THE PURPOSE OF PRESENTING THE ART OF THE FIRST AMERICANS AS FINE ART. ASIDE FROM EXPLANATORY COMMENT THE BOOK STANDS, THEN, AS A SUPPLEMENTAL EXHIBIT OF THE REDMAN'S AESTHETICS, GIVING EXAMPLES OF WOVEN AND COLORFUL PHRASES PROPER TO THE SPLENDID COMPANY OF HIS FINE TEXTILES, FINE CERAMICS AND EXQUISITE SIMPLICITIES IN PAINTING AND SCULPTURE.

NOW WHEN THE WHITE MAN'S INTRODUCED CIVILIZATION FALTERS BEFORE A GLUT OF FOOD AND A LAPSE OF ETHICS THE OLD AMERICAN CIVILIZATION OF PRE-COLUMBIAN DAYS HOLDS LESSONS NOT TO BE IGNORED. THE REDMAN'S SOCIAL RESTRAINTS KEPT THE RESOURCES OF THE NEW WORLD INTACT AGAINST OUR COMING. HIS DISTINGUISHED SKILL SET UP SOME OF THE BEST STANDARDS OF CRAFTSMANSHIP. HIS PATIENT HUSBANDRY WON FOR US OUR MOST IMPORTANT CROPS. BETTER STILL HE DEMONSTRATED THAT UPON A WISE USE OF LEISURE SAVED FROM THE PURSUIT OF FOOD AND MERE NECESSITIES REST THOSE INTELLECTUAL, ARTISTIC AND RELIGIOUS COMMONWEALTHS WHICH ARE THE CROWN AND GLORY OF MANKIND.

AFTER THE MANNER OF ANCIENT AMERICA OUR PRESENT SOCIETY SHOULD FIND AN INCREASING PROPORTION OF ITS MEMBERS ENGAGED IN CULTURAL EMPLOYMENT. YET TODAY, SUFFERING FROM TOO MUCH GOOD FORTUNE, WE CURTAIL ART, SCIENCE AND EDUCATION AND BEND EVERY EFFORT TO STIMULATE A SPENDTHRIFT DESTRUCTION OF NATURAL WEALTH IN THE NAME OF BUSINESS AND INDUSTRY. OUR INDIANS OF THE PAST CHALLENGE THE VALIDITY OF OUR SOCIAL PURPOSES.

PREFACE

H.J. Spinden: A Recollection
by Alice Marriott

It may not be that there were giants on the earth in the early days of anthropology in the United States, but, viewed from the perspective of three-quarters of a century, the founding fathers of our discipline seem men of gigantic stature.

In those days a Doctor of Philosophy was held to be a man of learning who had acquired and enriched a philosophy of his own – a man of learning, not of barren erudition. Unlike Browning's "Grammarian," he did not narrow his knowledge to the modifiers of a single Greek verb but allowed it to spread and flourish widely, available to all who wished to share it.

Such a man was Herbert Joseph Spinden. It is as impossible to think of Spinden's speaking of "My Tewa" or "My Aztecs" as it is to think of Franz Boas referring to "My Kwakiutl" or John Swanton's saying "My Creeks." The professional jargon of our day, which allows an ethnologist, now usually a specialist, to claim "My Cheyennes" or "My Hopis," had not been coined in Spinden's day.

A look at the introductory essay in this volume will bear this out. The writer covers not only the whole field of American Indian linguistics and poetry but ranges freely from Peru to Baffin and quotes with equal fluidity and point from Inca and Eskimo alike, with asides to representative intermediate peoples.

It has been asked how many American Indian languages Spinden spoke. The actual number does not matter. He learned what he needed of speech, rhythm and construction. Above all he was convinced that poetry, whatever its language, was a matter of feeling and of expression of feeling. Words were secondary in meaning.

Spinden will probably be best remembered for his great controversy with Sylvanus G. Morley over Maya date glyphs, a battle which raged for years and is still being carried on by the disciples of the prophets. It is unfortunate that two men of such intelligence, charm, and humanitarianism should be remembered most for a negative, and sometimes almost petty argument. For when one thinks of Dr. Spinden -- Uncle Joe, Tio Pepe, whatever one might call him -- in his absence, it is the warmth of the man one remembers. Sitting with René and Sarah d' Harnoncourt in their living room on Russian Hill and watching lights come out around San Francisco Bay, sipping a glass of sherry, and hearing him say, "One can believe in Elysian Fields at times like this," or coming into Bella Weitzner's office at the American Museum, and having the bulk hunched over her desk turn at the sound of a remembered voice, "My dear! I can't see you, but how good to hear you speak!"

One thinks of him in earlier years, in the Brooklyn Museum, patiently counting pre-Columbian threads with Theresa Goell, and breaking off to take everyone available to lunch. Even after his vision was almost gone he still haunted museums. Policemen herded him through the intersection of Fifth Avenue and 42nd Street, to and from the New York Public Library, where he sat for hours at a table full of reference books before undertaking the subway journey back to Brooklyn.

It seems natural enough for one woman to think of Dr. Spinden in connection with other women. He was one of those rare men who truly enjoy women. Some he loved, but many more he liked and respected; with whom he shared ideas and battles of ideas. Not that he lacked for men friends – and combatants. His contemporaries: Kidder, Tozzer, Nusbaum, Mason, Hewett and Morley were only a few of them. Younger men were his friends, too: Douglas and d'Harnoncourt, Bird and Barrett, Ford and Eckholm -- all of them in some way associated with museum work. He stimulated them, furnished information and ideas and leads to obscure sources he had discovered in Middle America.

The years between 1907 and 1910 were busy ones for anthropologists in the Southwest. In 1907 Edgar Lee Hewett started the series of excavations on the Pajarito Plateau, northwest of Santa Fe, New Mexico, which laid the foundations for systematic study of Anasazi and Pueblo cultures. Almost all of the older men we have mentioned participated in these digs, and Maria and Julian Martinez of San Ildefonso Pueblo were there, too, and began their experiments in reconstructing Pueblo potteries from sherds that Hewett brought to them.

Dr. Spinden was in the Southwest in those years, but his interest at that time was more ethnological and linguistic than archaeological. Archaeology, for him, came later. He spent much time in the Tewa villages: Nambe, San Ildefonso, Santa Clara, San Juan and Teseque. In the course of his field work, Spinden recorded linguistic texts, some of which are still to be translated. It was a labor of love, and a hard and valuable one, for languages, as Spinden was well aware, are flexible things, and change with speaking. It is safe to say that the Tewa spoken at Nambe today is vastly different from that used a generation or two ago. And Tewa is on its way out now, being replaced by Spanish and English. One wonders if it will survive another hundred years as a spoken language.

The years between 1914 and 1926 marked the low point in North American Indian cultures. There was war in Europe, and in time the United States was drawn into it. In 1924 Congress bestowed United States citizenship on all Indians as a token of gratitude for their services in World War I. Voting rights, established by the states, came later -- in most cases *much* later.

In 1926 conditions among Indians had reached their all-time low. The Merriam Commission of the Institute for Government Research (usually referred to as the Brookings Institution, named after the Chairman of the Board of Trustees) was asked by Congress to investigate and report on the situation. For one year a group of educators, historians, anthropologists, economists and medical personnel traveled through the reservations and the non-reservation area of Oklahoma. The report they drew up and submitted to the government was voluminous and horrifying. Indians lived in sickness, poverty, filth and ignorance in the midst of a country that prided itself on abolishing such things.

Spinden was out of the country during this period. He returned in 1930 and was immediately drawn into the conscious movement to establish a responsible place for the American Indians. One feature of the movement was the American Indian Tribal Arts Exposition, set up on Madison Avenue, New York City. Here the finest crafts work of past and present was gathered for display and sale to the general public. Another feature of the Exposition was a series of pamphlets on different facets of American Indian life. For one of these Spinden retranslated and edited his notes on Tewa songs and American Indian poetry. He also contributed pamphlets on Fine Arts and the American Indian and on Indian symbolism.

Inevitably, the accent of the Exposition was on the Southwest, particularly on New Mexico. Mary Austin, Alice Corbin Henderson, E.W. Gifford, and Margaretta Dietrich all contributed papers to the pamphlet series. Others, like Mary Wheelwright, Amelia Elizabeth White, Leslie Van Ness Denman, and Mrs. Dietrich contributed funds that made it possible to set up displays and print pamphlets. It was certainly a non-profit organization. Under the combined pressures of a Democratic administration and a world-wide depression, it went, as the Indian say, underground. But the Exposition bore fruit that is still growing. The Indian Arts and Crafts Board of the Department of the Interior was established under Secretary Ickes and still functions as an education and sales medium throughout the United States and, with the assistance of the State Department, abroad.

Many of the originators of the American Indian Exposition worked with the Arts and Crafts Board as advisors and consultants, and, in case of necessity, as angels. Through their public relations – highly individualized, it is true -- they made possible two milestones in museum display: The Indian display at the Pan-Pacific Exposition in San Francisco in 1939 and the even more magnificent "Indian Arts of the United States" at the Museum of Modern Art in New York City in January of 1941. Display techniques developed and perfected in these two expeditions are still in use.

And Spinden was right there and in action. He buzzed -- always monolithic in a great overcoat, as one remembers -- back and forth from coast to coast. He induced museums to lend specimens that had never been displayed before. He lectured, and sometimes, when there was nothing else to do, he wrote -- usually letters. One wonders how many are drying out in files over the country.

Spinden was not a man to suffer fools gladly. He was god-like in his contempt for those who asked too many personal questions. If he wanted to reminisce about Maya ruins, he did so, but any biographical information was incidental to the method of carving glyphs.

Biographical material on Spinden is scarce. Much of the time he worked in parts of the hemisphere where mail was erratic, and months might pass between the mailing of a biographical questionnaire and its receipt. More months would pass before the papers could be returned, if they were returned at all.

Herbert Spinden was a man who valued his privacy, and biographical facts about him that are available are few.

He was born August 16, 1879, in Huron, South Dakota. Presumably he was educated locally until he matriculated at Harvard University in 1902. He received his B.A. there in 1906, his M.A. in 1908, and his Ph.D. in 1909.

Much of his time was spent in field work, but he compiled an impressive list of positions. From 1909 to 1921 he was Assistant Curator of Anthropology at the American Museum of Natural History in New York City. From 1921 to 1926 he was Curator of Mexican Archaeology at Harvard's Peabody Museum and from 1926 to 1929 was Curator of Archaeology at the Buffalo, New York, Museum. After that he became Curator of American Indian Art and Primitive Cultures at the Brooklyn Museum, a position he held until his retirement in 1951.

It is almost impossible to compile a Spinden bibliography. Many of his works are out of print; others appeared in obscure or highly-specialized journals and bulletins. His greatest work was The Maya Calendar, an offshoot of his Ph.D. dissertation. Next in importance is Maya Art, published in 1913.

Dr. Spinden was President of the American Anthropological Association, the Eastern Association on Indian Affairs, and the Explorers Club. With how many other learned societies he was associated in one capacity or another would be hard to guess.

Certainly his great, bulky figure, his shock of white hair, and his piercing blue eyes — Siamese cat eyes, someone once called them — were a part of the American anthropological scene for many years, until his death at Castle Point Hospital in Cold Springs, where he had been taken from his home in Carmel, New York, October 26, 1967, at the age of 88.

Dr. Spinden spanned the history of anthropology in North America. He lived to see his work destructively criticized, and he lived to see it examined and reexamined, and finally accepted. No man could ask for more, especially no man who enjoyed a good fight.

Anthropologists are necrologists by nature, intent and training. Why obituaries of Spinden's contemporaries should be abundant and sometimes wordy in professional journals, while none of him was published, is a mystery. Did his fight with Morley and his followers carry beyond the graves of both men? Or was it his often-stated conviction that "the work was more important than the worker" influenced those who might have written about him? Such questions must go unanswered for the present. One would like to write fully of the man as well as of his work, but the cover to that volume remains closed.

INTRODUCTION

When this new printing of SONGS OF THE TEWA was being prepared I was asked to write a short introduction in order "to bring things up to date." Any work published over forty years ago usually needs some explanation to justify its reprinting. A quick reading of Dr. Spinden's text showed me that my job was all but unnecessary. A good part of this book could have been written within the last year. Spinden's cry against the wanton destruction of our natural resources and wild life, written in 1933, sounds all too familiar to the ecologists of 1975.

Only one of the author's statements no longer holds true, and no one would be more pleased, I am sure, than Dr. Spinden to discover this change. In the early thirties he wrote that Indian poets tend to anonymity; that Indian poetry lacks the individual viewpoint. For centuries the American Indian literary tradition was primarily an oral one. Since written languages were rare among native North and South American cultures, all literature - myth, legend, story, poetry - was passed along the generations through memory and the spoken word. This lack of written languages plus the communal society of most tribes tended to encourage this cultural anonymity. It was not until the second quarter of the 20th century that Indian artists and craftsmen began to sign their work with any regularity, and this was done in most cases at the insistence of White traders and dealers.

In the few short years since Spinden's death, however, a new generation of American Indians has emerged. Politically astute, frequently militant and increasingly outspoken, these "new" Indians have entered the mainstream of American life. During the past ten years an American Indian has won the Pulitzer Prize for fiction. At the same time Indian poets have begun to be published as individuals. The Indian writer, in other words, has come out of the anthropological closet; has left behind his audience of scholars and has reached for a broader public.

Dr. Spinden collected at a time when the Indian poetic voice was still a nameless one. The songs included here are of that period; they are the source and the heritage. Without them present and future Indian poetry could not be. Without an understanding and appreciation of them present and future Indian poetry will have little meaning.

Wm. Farrington
Santa Fe, New Mexico
September, 1975

Portrait of Spinden.

AN ESSAY ON
AMERICAN INDIAN POETRY

with a selection of outstanding compositions
from North and South America

A GIFT of noble art in all its manifestations, destined to gather golden opinions with the passing centuries, forms part of the splendid heritage with which America of the past endows America of the future. The Redman has never received the credit due him for his fundamental contributions to human welfare and permanent civilization. On the utilitarian side stand the remarkable series of economic plants which the Indian brought to a high state of cultivation and the important industrial processes which he invented. On the esthetic side stand beauty in sculpture and architecture, beauty in traditional literature of myths, songs and ritualistic poems, beauty in dances and spectacular ceremonies, and beauty, above all, in the ethical and philosophical attitude of man towards man and of man towards nature.

It is easy enough to show that the useful gifts of the American Indian assume gigantic values today, especially since more than half the present agricultural wealth of the United States comes from plants which he tamed. It is not so easy to estimate the influence of his esthetics upon the present culture of his conquerors, but the coming effect will surely be very great. The Indian has abundantly demonstrated his ability to build up and maintain the social illusions of grandeur. Now between a nation which exists as an accumulation of individual abilities and individual achievements—and we are scarcely more than this today in spite of a certain mechanistic ordering—and a nation which finds a truly artistic and communal expression of its cooperative life,

capable of enriching and ennobling that life, there is a
vast and vital difference. Perhaps in this survey of the
poetry of the American Indian I shall be able to define
this difference in comprehensive terms.

The creative individuals of the Red race, the poets,
the artists, the philosophers, whatever their forgotten
names may be, had this in common: they were one and
all the architects of mass illusion. They were culture
heroes, and to my mind this is the highest purpose to
which supreme abilities may be devoted. Seeing in the
realities of the world about them the indices of divine
intention, their minds reached out to win an invisible
empire. Although possessing separate abilities they were
not individualists in spirit but collectivists, and the
self-contained societies which they erected were super-
organisms instinct with over-souls.

Perhaps the cultural units of ancient America repre-
sent primary or youthful civilization. Such a classifica-
tion would well fit the first splendid efflorescence of the
Mayas which produced writing, astronomical science,
permanent architecture and high art. Here, if ever, we
find self-sufficiency, a nation growing like a tree. For the
Mayas drew wealth from their own soil and developed
their supreme arts by an intelligent use of leisure in
furtherance of their social ideals. It seems that the same
process was repeated elsewhere in America. But also it is
clear enough that the Incas and the Aztecs had hit upon
the deceptive advantages of aggressive warfare in the
quick up-building of their respective states. Their
predatory policy was still tentative, for the undeveloped
condition of both offensive and defensive military
science among the American Indians in general proves
that the procedures of conquest, tribute and trade were
never fully established. The Redman had to dance

himself into war or find a just cause for it in the imagined appetites of his gods.

THE INDIAN AND HIS COSMOS

In his relations with the immeasurable world about him the American Indian, even today and whatever the state of his culture, exhibits a single psychological attitude. Man is never the lord of creation but always a pensioner on natural bounty. It has been the custom to dismiss the religion of our Indian tribes as animistic in the lower stages and mystic in the higher ones, a classification which certainly emphasizes the supremacy of spiritual forces over material ones. Beginning with a naive belief that a directive mentality combines with a directed physical body in animals, plants and natural objects as it does in man, the first aim of Indian religion has been to make friends with nature whenever possible and when not possible to circumvent in some way the inimical forces. From this universal animism beast gods emerge as the embodiments of natural powers. Ultimately these beast gods combine into composite monster gods which gradually take on human attributes of shape and character. But very early in the development of this system the idea of a single pervasive control makes its appearance, a primal cause, a creator, a modifier, who may deal out rewards as well as punishments.

The Yokuts Indian of California, after appealing to seven vague deities whom he names in order, ends with the request that he may fit into a universal scheme[1].

My words are tied in one
With the great mountains,
With the great rocks,
With the great trees,
In one with my body
And my heart.

Do you all help me
With supernatural power,
And you, Day
And you, Night!
All of you see me
One with this world!

In a closing comment on this primitive Californian prayer, Kroeber says: "A certain vastness of conception and profoundness of feeling rising above any petty concrete desire, cannot be denied this petition."

Out on the Great Plains the mystery which pervades the universe is called Wakonda by several Siouan tribes. The quest of Wakonda by the man who would know things "that are fit to serve as symbols" is thus described in the Osage Rite of the Chiefs[2]:

> In the midst of the open prairie, where trees grow not,
> As he sat upon the earth to rest he thought: This spot, also,
>   may be Wakonda's abode!
> Then he inclined his head towards his right side,
> Bent his body low,
> And Wakonda made him close his eyes in sleep.

From the Osage informant who gave Francis La Flesche the important rituals of this tribe comes an explanation of Wakonda[3]. It was the ancients who devised the ritualistic songs, the ceremonial forms and symbols out of their insight into natural mysteries, arising from their power to search with the mind. They noted the "mysteries of the light of day by which the earth and all living things that dwell thereon are influenced; the mysteries of the darkness of night that reveal to us all the great bodies of the upper world, each of which forever travels in a circle upon its own path unimpeded by the others. They searched for a long period of time for the source of life and at last came to the thought that it issues from an invisible creative power to which they applied the name Wakonda." This from one American Indian to another!

Wakonda and his congeners—for the name varies with the language—resides in the heavens and sometimes appears to his petitioners in human guise, but aged and austere. In literature dealing with the Indian he is generally referred to as the Great Mystery but he might with equal propriety be called Ultimate Good.

The Pueblo Indians of the Southwest speak of their Earth Mother and Sky Father and in a chant of the Tewa (see number XXIX below) ask for a garment to be woven on the gossamer loom, strung from the sky by the desert rains, that they may walk fittingly in a decent world. If only our materialistic civilizations now stripping the earth in a mad holocaust could pause and take counsel from the calm wisdom of this prayer! But it seems that we accept no lesson from the past and owe no duty to the future. The destruction of forests and all natural resources goes on, the flocks of wild birds and herds of wild animals die and we pollute the streams. Enslaving or exterminating undefended peoples around the world we enslave ourselves to sordid appetites and disillusions.

The Aztecs had a vague supreme deity called Ome-teuctli—Lord of Duality—who combined the masculine and feminine principles in one creator god dwelling in a topmost heaven.

Nezahualcoyotl, the emperor-poet of Texcoco, is credited by the Mexican historian, Ixtlilxochitl, with having taught that there was one god supreme above all others named Tloque Nahuaque: "In the ninth tier was the creator of heaven and earth, by whom live the created beings: an only god who created all visible and invisible things." This most famous poet of ancient Mexico also realized the ethical implications of this reduction in his emphasis on just deeds as the proper worship to be offered to an eternal principle. In a poem intended to be sung in his presence we find these verses[4]:

Little will fame have to tell of this wondrous majesty,
worthy of a thousand heralds, the nations will only re-
member how wisely governed the three chieftains who held
the power.

At Mexico Montezuma the famous and valorous, at Culhua-
can the fortunate Nezahualcoyotl, and at the stronghold of
Acatlapan, Totoquilhuatli.

I fear no oblivion for thy just deeds, standing as thou dost
in thy place appointed by the Supreme Lord of All, who
governs all things.

A most splendid Thanatopsis, attributed to Neza-
hualcoyotl, comes to us through an Otomi transcription,
offering internal evidence of its pagan origin. I quote the
English rendering of Brinton[5]. While faltering here and
there in exact phrasing, nevertheless the early American-
ist caught the vast scope of this poem. It expresses, as
he says, an epicurean philosophy but one permeated
by ethical obligations.

1. The fleeting pomps of the world are like the green willow
trees, which aspiring to permanence, are consumed by a fire,
fall before the axe, are upturned by the wind, or are scarred
and saddened by age.

2. The grandeurs of life are like the flowers in color and in
fate; the beauty of these remains so long as their chaste buds
gather and store the rich pearls of the dawn and saving it,
drop it in liquid dew; but scarcely has the Cause of All
directed upon them the full rays of the sun, when their
beauty and glory fail, and the brilliant gay colors which
decked forth their pride wither and fade.

3. The delicious realms of flowers count their dynasties by
short periods; those which in the morning revel proudly in
beauty and strength, by evening weep for the sad destruction
of their thrones, and for the mishaps which drive them to
loss, to poverty, to death and to the grave. All things of
earth have an end, and in the midst of the most joyous lives,
the breath falters, they fall, they sink into the ground.

4. All the earth is a grave, and nought escapes it; nothing is
so perfect that it does not fall and disappear. The rivers,
brooks, fountains and waters flow on, and never return to
their joyous beginnings; they hasten on to the vast realms of
Tlaloc, and the wider they spread between their marges the

more rapidly do they mould their own sepulchral urns. That which was yesterday is not today; and let not that which is today trust to live tomorrow.

5. The caverns of earth are filled with pestilential dust which once was the bones, the flesh, the bodies of great ones who sat upon thrones, deciding causes, ruling assemblies, governing armies, conquering provinces, possessing treasures, tearing down temples, flattering themselves with pride, majesty, fortune, praise and dominion. These glories have passed like the dark smoke thrown out by the fires of Popocatepetl, leaving no monuments but the rude skins on which they are written.

6. Ha! ha! Were I to introduce you into the obscure bowels of this temple, and were to ask you which of these bones were those of the powerful Achalchiuhtlanextin, first chief of the ancient Toltecs; of Necaxecmitl, devout worshipper of the gods; if I inquire where is the peerless beauty of the glorious empress Xiuhtzal, where the peaceable Topiltzin, last monarch of the hapless land of Tulan; if I ask you where are the sacred ashes of our first father Xolotl; those of the bounteous Nopal; those of the generous Tlotzin; or even the still warm cinders of my glorious and immortal, though unhappy and luckless father Ixtlilxochitl; if I continued thus questioning about all our august ancestors, what would you reply? The same that I reply—I know not. I know not; for first and last are confounded in the common clay. What was their fate shall be ours, and of all who follow us.

7. Unconquered princes, warlike chieftains, let us seek, let us sigh for the heaven, for there all is eternal, and nothing is corruptible. The darkness of the sepulchre is but the strengthening couch for the glorious sun, and the obscurity of the night but serves to reveal the brilliancy of the stars. No one has power to alter these heavenly lights, for they serve to display the greatness of their Creator, and as our eyes see them now, so saw them our earliest ancestors, and so shall see them our latest posterity.

The human soul lost in the immensities of a space-time universe has no recourse from oblivion save in those virtues which blossom in the dust. This is the conclusion of the highest paganism. Seeing order in the heavens instills a belief that there may be an ultimate order in the solution of human affairs.

In conformity with the reflections of the great Mexican chieftain are various ancient hymns and ora-

tions which are ascribed to the kings of the Incas by
one Joan de Santa Cruz Pachacuti Yamqui Salcamaygua
who wrote shortly after 1600. The hymn to Viracocha,
a master deity and creator god of Peru, is an oft-quoted
fragment of American Indian literature[6].

> O Viracocha, Lord of the Universe,
> Whether Thou be male or female
> At least lord of heat and generation!
> O such a one as can divine with spittle,
> Where art Thou?
> If only Thou wert near thy son!
>
> Thou mayest be above,
> Thou mayest be below,
> Or round about Thy rich throne or staff.
> O listen to me!
>
> From the sea above in which Thou mayest dwell,
> From the sea below in which Thou mayest be,
> Creator of the world,
> Maker of man,
> Lord of all lords!
>
> With my eyes on Thee which fail to see Thee
> Yet desiring to know Thee!
> Might I behold Thee,
> Know Thee,
> Consider Thee,
> Understand Thee!
> For Thou beholdest me,
> Knowest me!
>
> The Sun, the Moon
> The Day, the Night
> Summer, Winter
> Not vainly, in proper order,
> Do they march to the destined place,
> To the end!
> They arrive wherever Thy royal staff
> Thou bearest.
> Hear me!
> Heed me!
> Let it not happen
> That I grow tired,
> That I die!

So all prefiguring of space and time draws down to the focus of human needs, of human understanding, and of human recognition of something that goes beyond this understanding! Man is the animal who learned to wonder, who learned to question the world, who learned to question himself. Through the length and breadth of ancient America we discover this primitive inquisitiveness and even in the songs of our Indians of today. Here is one from the Pawnee[7]:

> Let me see, if this be real,
> Let me see, if this be real,
> Let me see, if this be real,
> Let me see, if this be real,
> This life I am living?
> Ye who possess the skies,
> Let me see if this be real,
> This life I am living.

THE PLACE OF INDIAN POETRY
IN THE ARTS

"ALL POETRY," says Grosse[8], "comes from feeling and goes to feeling, and therein lies the mystery of its creation and influence." This writer of forty years ago did not have much truly primitive poetry before him nor did he have much sensitive knowledge of the uses to which that little had been applied in the life of primitive man. His basic definition, "Poetry is the verbal representation of external or internal phenomena in an esthetically effective form for an esthetic purpose," implied that the successful uses of words to express great thoughts and tender feelings were, from the first, intentional creations of specially gifted artists. But was this really the case?

Today, as a result of ethnological studies among nearly all the surviving groups of low-cultured humans, we have masses of traditional myths, songs and ritual-

istic proceedings. The native forms of speech have been
written out phonetically, translated in the light of local
associations, and coordinated with the rhythms of
musical accompaniment and with the ordered action of
dancing and ceremonial dramatizations in sound-and-
sight records. This slow and searching investigation has
proceeded without undue benefit from *a priori* considera-
tions and without undue loyalty to slender and precious
definitions of what distinguishes Art in a matrix of
Custom.

The idea that the separate fine arts sprang full-armed
from the brow of, let us say, Apollo and that artists
were, in the beginning or ever, touched with divine
afflatus has no more truth in it than the companion con-
cept that kings operate under a heavenly sanction.
Anthropological science can demonstrate easily enough
that beauty emerges from use, and that many ancient
things which according to our specialized appreciations
are merely and completely beautiful were nevertheless
conceived for some magical or pseudo-practical service.

Poetry can hardly be called a primary art, at least
that class of it which needs only to be spoken or read.
As used by the American Indians and other so-called
primitive groups, such as the Polynesians, poetry is
still a servant of music and ceremony rather than a free-
standing utterance. Perhaps this was also its former
state in those classic lands where lyrics no longer need
the lyre and where ballads are seldom actually sung to
dancing feet. Owing to the lack of stringed instruments
in ancient America and the slight development of wind
instruments the drum exerted an outstanding influence
on song, with some help from the steady pulsations of
canoe paddling, corn grinding and similar exercises.

Among the Eskimo is found the Arctic tambourine

and throughout the New World drums of one kind or
another are in use. In ancient Mexico the two-lipped log
drum had a double pitch and was capable of producing
a wide variety of sound patterns through manipulation
of the double tones in light and heavy strokes and
changing tempo[9]. We must imagine that melodic meas-
ures coincided with these drum beats and furnished a
still more intricate lay-out into which it was the poet's
job to fit intelligible words. The drum rhythms are
indicated imitatively for a considerable number of old
Mexican songs and their variety may be guessed from
three examples[10]. While the iambic meter goes especially
well with the Aztec language, other meters were also
employed: else how can the following onomatopoeia of
drum strokes be explained?

> Tico, tico, toco toto, and as the song approached the end,
> tiqui, titi, tito, titi.
>   *   *   *
>
> Quititi, quititi, quiti, tocoto, tocoti, tocoto, tocoti, and
> then it is to turn back again.
>   *   *   *
>
> Toto, tiquiti, tiquiti, and then it ends, tocotico, tocoti,
> toto, titiqui, toto, titiquiti.

Modern examples of the ways in which words are
forced into inflexible moulds of music have been studied
in phonographic records of songs from the Eskimo, the
Ojibwa and other tribes. Often the distortion is so great
that a song has meaning only for the composer. The
expression may be obscure enough in itself with far-
fetched figures of speech and various poetic licenses. On
top of this the warping of the words to the rhythmic
pattern sometimes calls for drastic syncopations and re-
duplications, not to mention the interpolation of
meaningless syllables. Poetry schooled under such rigid
restraints, and finally overcoming them, inevitably be-

comes differentiated from prose. There is a survival of the
fittest expressions until a standard of poetic phrasing
becomes fixed.

The common use of extra, meaningless syllables to
dilute the intelligible parts of speech is illustrated in a
Mide song of the Ojibwa analyzed by Miss Densmore.
The words are[11]:

Ni wá waké aboǵ	A bubbling spring
We wendjí dji wûñ'	Comes from the hard ground.

The pulse of the drum is regular and the quarter note
is maintained except for the fifth and sixth measures.
To fit a combination of 2-4, 3-4 and 4-4 time the words
of the song are repeated and stretched out as follows,
the italicised syllables being interpolated.

....Wac	ke a bog	*o ho ho* ni
wa *a* ac	ke a bog	*o ho ho ho ho ho ho ho* ni
wa *ha ha*	wac ke a bog	*o ho ho* ni
wa *ha ha*	wac ke a bog	*o ho ho* ni
wa *a* ac	ke a bog	*o ho ho* ni
wa *a a*	wac ke a bog	*o ho ho*
we wen	dji dji wuñ	*e he he*
we wen	dji dji wuñ	*e he he he* ne
wa *ha ha*	wac ke a bog	*o ho ho* ni

There are many songs in which the burden is carried
entirely by meaningless syllables but it is not clear that
such songs intergrade as a class between instrumental
music and songs with intelligible words. In some cases
the meaningless syllables may represent old songs, the
words of which have been distorted and forgotten, or
foreign songs, the words of which never were learned.
It would help if we could really measure the life of a
song. We only know that the rich repertory of the
Aztecs and the Incas has been finished for centuries and
that long life in an unmodified state cannot be proven

for European ballads. Yet there is a common belief that
the songs and ceremonies of lowly cultured peoples are
maintained from ancient times. "The Amazonian," says
Thomas Whiffen[12], "treasures the songs of his fathers and
will master strange rhythms and words that for him no
longer have meaning; he only knows they are the correct
lines, the phrases he ought to sing at such functions,
because they have always been sung." This assumption
of longevity for traditional songs is, I believe, nothing
more than a romantic exit for ignorance. Rather, it
seems that generations of song and ceremony succeeded
each other like generations of human beings, albeit with
a longer natural life, and that survival of traits, or at
best survival of broken fragments, is all that should be
expected across a span of several centuries. A constant
process of leavening the present with the past is sufficient
to explain all certain facts.

Words adjusted to the metronome of the throbbing
drum, or embodying a rhythmic formality once removed,
were composed by the American Indians for various
purposes and occasions. Many songs were framed for the
uses of magic, others to vivify ceremonies, others to
express the deep religious feelings of the social group.
Relatively few Indian poems have the strictly individual-
istic cast which distinguishes so many products of our
super-civilized nation. It seems that Indian singers did
not consciously cultivate the violent personal emotions
for the trade, but ventured only to put into words the
social illusions in which they were immersed. Now to
examine the outstanding classes of Indian poetical
compositions.

REINCARNATION LULLABIES

INDIAN MOTHERS generally sing their children to sleep
with wordless songs but sometimes they use true lulla-

bies as may be seen from the Tewa examples given below. There is, moreover, a very special kind of lullaby which deals with reincarnation.

The Eskimo and several other northern tribes believe that the soul of a dead relative enters into a new born child and watches over it during its tender years. This person may be addressed, therefore, in the child's lullaby and, vice versa, the child's prattling tongue may drop words of wisdom, thanks to its experienced soul. While the lullabies of eastern Greenland, which Thalbitzer calls petting songs, are of this type they mostly lack artistic form and some are frankly licentious, ascribing to the infant child the vices and ailments of its spiritual tutor, perhaps as preventive magic. There are a few exceptions. A widow whose dead husband had entered into his brother's son saw in this male child her future provider, and addressed him with a song more befitting our idea of what a lullaby should be. I quote the first of three similar verses[13]:

> How bland he is and gentle, the great little one there!
> How bland he is and gentle—
> How amazing he is, the dear little creature!

Among the Tlingit of southern Alaska and the Haida of Queen Charlotte Island are found reincarnation lullabies of dignified phrasing which Swanton has translated[14]. One such song apologizes for the mean life of the present as compared with the exalted past; it is addressed to an old woman whose spiritual personality continues its existence in a baby girl.

I

> You need not think that the smoke of your house in the middle of Skeedans will be as great as when you were a woman.
>
> II
>
> You need not think they will make a continual noise of singing in Skeedans Creek as they used to when you were a woman.

In still another reincarnation lullaby the fond mother beholds a famous chieftain in her crawling infant.

I

He says it is Nañkilslas's great father moving along so greatly—
Halloo, great chief moving about!

II

Halloo, he moves along greatly like something extending to the sky.
Halloo, great chief moving about!

We must now note that as the child grows older his proper soul gradually gets control over the body and the reincarnated adult soul fades away into nothingness. So these northern peoples also have other songs fitted to the understanding of little boys and girls. For instance the Ammassalik Eskimo have a myth for children which tells how a raven teased the geese and how the geese in revenge enticed the raven far out over the sea. When they settled on the water, he was unable to swim. A song describes his fate[15]:

Halloo, I sink, help me up, Ugh!
Now the water reaches my great ankles,
Halloo, I sink, help me up, Ugh!
Now it reaches my great knees.
Halloo, I sink, help me up; Uhg!
Now it reaches my great groins
Halloo, I sink, help me up, Ugh!
Now it reaches my great navel
Halloo, I sink, help me up, Ugh!
Now it reaches my great breasts
Halloo, I sink, help me up, Ugh!

And so on until the water reaches the great eyes of the insolent raven; then the song ends with an expressive Ugh!
Elsewhere songs for children and songs in myths which are used largely in the education of children

emphasize the magical factor. A selection of songs for children from the village of Picuris in New Mexico has been published by John P. Harrington and Helen Roberts[16]. A story tells how a child-stealing giant is overcome by a youth's magical songs. The boy's first song sung while he is being carried away in a basket, ends with the phrase:

A person who is very kind is carrying me on his back.

This has the magical effect of increasing the load and tiring out the giant. Later when the giant covers the youth with pitch and throws him in the fire a second song is sung the burden of which is:

A person who is very kind has put me in a warm place.

This has the magical effect of lulling the giant to sleep and the youth steps out of the fire and kills him. The point of this tale is that songs are more potent than common prose, a lesson which the Indian carries through life.

GUARDIAN SPIRIT SONGS

INDIAN BOYS of many tribes, and sometimes girls as well, were accustomed to pass through the supreme experience of having revealed to them in a vision a guardian spirit, their special link with the mystical hinterworld. The oldest and best songs of the Plains tribes are said to have been "composed in dreams" and Miss Frances Densmore thinks that this is only the Indian's way of expressing what we mean by "poetic inspiration." But there was perhaps more method in the Redman's madness.

The Indian youth sought his vision with hope and faith, keeping a lonely vigil till common realities faded and subconscious desires became manifest as spiritual realities. The guardian spirit song of one of my old

Nez Percé friends was a vividly descriptive phrase or two
set up in the midst of meaningless syllables. His vision
revealed Coyote returning from successful warfare and
the intelligible part of the song ran as follows:

> Ravening Coyote comes,
> red hands, red mouth,
> necklace of eye-balls!

The man's sacred name was Silu-we-haikt which
means Eyes-Around-the-Neck. The dream song was
first revealed by the dreamer in the annual Guardian
Spirit Dance where each dancer costumed himself
according to the nature of his vision. Guardian spirit
songs could be inherited and so might pass into a tribal
thesaurus of poetic expressions. There was undoubtedly
a bond between persons with the same protecting
animal, a fact of interest in relation to the origin of
totemic clans and esoteric societies. Among the Nez
Percé, where neither clans nor warriors' societies had
developed, there was an unusual number of mad coyote
songs, the result of visions which ensured military
success. One ran about like this:

> Mad Coyote,
> madly sings,
> then roars the west wind!

and another:

> Day break finds me,
> eastern day break finds me
> the meaning of that song:
> with blood-stained mouth,
> comes mad Coyote!

Among the Teton Sioux the men who had the
unusual success of obtaining a Thunder-bird vision fell
in a special group called Heyoka and at certain times had

to express themselves in an opposite fashion from normal people. Lone Man of this tribe put on record the details of his vision and the four songs given him by the Thunder-bird people who appeared as horsemen in the clouds. The last one can be arranged as follows[17]:

> Friends, behold!
> sacred I have been made.
> Friends, behold!
> in a sacred manner I have been influenced.
> At the gathering of the clouds
> sacred I have been made.
> Friends, behold!
> sacred I have been made.

A Thunder-bird song of the Ojibwa seems to depart still farther from the realities of earth[18]:

> Sometimes
> I go pitying
> myself
> while I am carried by the wind
> across the sky.

Thunder-bird songs were also developed in connection with the Ghost Dance Religion which I discuss in another place. Such a piece from the Arapaho has always had for me a strong appeal[19]:

> My children, my children,
> It is I who make the thunder as I circle about—
>   The thunder as I circle about.
> My children, my children,
> It is I who make the loud thunder as I circle about
>   The loud thunder as I circle about.

Among some of the Plains tribes there were dream societies formed by men who had visions of the buffalo, the elk, the bear, etc., which were believed to convey special powers and faculties. Thus the men who dreamed of the bear had songs which helped in curing ceremonies.

The Land.

SONGS AS THE INSTRUMENTS OF MAGIC

Believing in the spirituality of plants, animals and even stones it is not surprising that the Indians found ways to make special appeals to the personalities in nature who exemplified special faculties and who might be induced to tutor man. Thus the Eskimo hunter sings[20]:

> What animal's sharp sight
> Have I for my sharp sight?
> The gull's sharp sight
> Have I for my sharp sight!

This song is not to be construed as a boast but as a petition. It seems that mere statement when made in the form of a song is compulsive. Indeed, "to sing" often means "to make magic," and back of it all lies the idea that the song has been ordained. The Pima put the matter thus[21]:

> Earth Magician now comes hither,
> Earth Magician now comes hither.
> From the depths the songs are rising
> And by him are here established.

The hunting animals sing their songs in myths and on inquiry it transpires that these same songs are re-sung by men who wish to have success in hunting.

Of course this procedure is merely an aspect of sympathetic magic in which descriptive words in a musical setting are held to be as potent as painted symbols in other circumstances. A myth of the Pawnee tells how a boy recovered a stolen robe bearing symbols of the storm, invoking the storm itself to destroy the thief. I quote a portion of this myth[22].

> The young man went through the village from one tipi to the other asking for his robe. The people had not seen it. At last he went up to the Witch-Woman and asked if she had

seen anything of his robe. She said: "No, I have not seen your robe." At the same time she made faces at the young man, saying to herself: "You will never find the robe. I now have it for a skirt." The young man went through the village again. He stood in the west, then walked through the village singing:

> I am hunting a robe.
> My painted robe I am hunting.
> The heavens are painted upon it.
> Attention! It is among the people.
> Attention! It is among the people.
> Attention! It is among the people.

When the old woman heard this she began to clap her hands and said: "The robe must be a wonderful one, but you shall never again have it in your hands, for the robe is my skirt." The boy sang again:

> I am hunting a robe.
> Who picked it up?
> Flocks of swallows are painted upon it . . .

When the woman heard it she said: "It must be a wonderful robe, but you shall never have it again, for I now have it for my skirt." The boy continued to sing:

> I am hunting a robe.
> Who has picked it up?
> Dragon-flies are painted upon it . . .

At last the boy began to sing:

> I am hunting a robe.
> Who has picked it up?
> The lightning is painted upon it . . .

> I am hunting a robe.
> Who has picked it up?
> The thunders are painted upon it . . .

> I am hunting a robe.
> Who has picked it up?
> The winds are painted upon it.
> Attention! It is among the people.
> Attention! It is among the people.
> Attention! It is among the people.

The Witch-Woman heard this song and she said: "Do you think I am going to be blown away when I have more power than you have?" The boy cried again. As he finished he blew his breath from the west to where the woman stood. Then he cried again and this time clouds were seen coming from the west. Clouds blew over the land. When the boy cried the fourth time the old woman took the robe off and threw it down and said: "My grandchild, there is your robe. You must not let the storm blow me away." Just about that time the wind caught the old woman and whirled her up into the heavens as if a whirlwind had struck her. It began to rain all over the land.

When we find in Indian poetry what seems to be an individual's emotional reaction to natural beauty, in keeping with our own romantic traditions, we should ask whether this is not a purposeful appreciation of the friendly aspects of nature in keeping with the Redman's philosophy that to imitate the way in which good is done is to insure the repetition of that good. For instance, take a Papago song recorded by Frances Densmore[23]:

By the sandy water I breathe the odor of the sea,
From there the wind comes and blows over the world.
By the sandy water I breathe the odor of the sea,
From there the clouds come and the rain falls over
the world.

To us these simple and majestic lines present a moving picture. From the given objective facts we construct some old experience and feel the immensity of the roaring ocean while storm racks pile up from below the horizon. Perhaps there comes over our minds a shadow of loneliness for we are accustomed to be sad in the presence of natural beauty—as though we had lost an animal birthright on getting civilized. We may even recall the similar lines which Gustavo Becquer wrote while starving in his garret in Madrid. But what a difference between the two songs when one scans the innermost sense. The first verse of Becquer's rhyme can be put in English as follows:

> Waves gigantic that break yourselves roaring
> On beaches deserted and distant,
> Wrapped in the sheet of the seafoam,
>   Carry me with you!

In this verse, and the three others that follow it, the German-Spanish romanticist dramatizes his personal despair.

Sometimes I think that individualism is only another social mode, and that it is made possible as a literary method by the psychic unity of mankind. Each person may find in himself a microcosm or miniature world and by correctly representing his own emotions discover a key to the macrocosm, or great world. Nevertheless the individualist goes through the motions of being anti-social, using society's words and society's conventions and shouting independence in accepted patterns through the bars of his prison cell. But the Papago song of the salt-gatherers is no enactment of personal joy or anguish but a rehearsing of nature's drama for the good that it may bring. This ulterior thought does not impair the validity of the esthetic experience and its proper expression any more than a fulfillment of function impairs the perfection of a wild rose. To be sure artificial cultivation for either a poem or a flower may proceed at the expense of function and end in sterile beauty.

It is difficult to say at what point beauty is recognized for itself alone, as a purely sensuous gratification. Of course, it is often possible to construe an Indian poem as a mere lyrical outburst. For instance, there is this one[24]:

> As my eyes search the prairie,
> I feel the summer in the spring.

Yet we are informed that this belongs in the magical category of dream songs.

By and large, the more backward tribes of both North and South America pay much attention to magic songs and some tribes possess little else. On the higher planes of culture the magical uses of poetry expand into great religious pieces. The Osage invocations to their sacred animals, patrons of tribal divisions, friends and benefactors of man are examples of this expansion. I quote the first and last passages in the *wi-gi-e* or introduction to the ceremony of incensing the seven sacred skins in the Rite of the Wa-xo-be. The lynx, the gray wolf, the puma, the black bear, the buffalo, the elk and finally the deer are set forth as symbols of courage[25].

> What shall the little ones make to be their symbol of courage as they travel the path of life? it has been said, in this house.
> The little mottled lynx that lies outstretched, they said,
> He who is their grandfather, a person of great courage, they shall make to be their symbol of courage, it has been said, in this house.
> At break of day
> My grandfather rushed forth to attack a deer with curved horns.
> My grandfather struck the deer and made it lie outstretched in death.
> My grandfather approached the fallen deer with an air of exultation;
> He gave a cry of triumph, and spake saying:
> When, towards the setting sun the little ones go forth to strike the enemy,
> In this manner they shall always triumph.
> Their hands shall ever be upon the foe, as they travel the path of life,
> Here he made a curve it is said in this house.
>
>   *   *   *   *   *
>
> What shall the little ones make to be the symbol of courage, as they travel the path of life? it has been said, in this house.
> The little animal that lies outstretched, they said,
> He who is their grandfather, although he has no gall,

They shall make to be their symbol of courage.
It was he who came upon four villages.
Close along their borders he ran swiftly without harm.
Even when he runs close to the borders of a village,
The arrows of his pursuers flying about him,
He escapes all dangers.
He it was who said: When the little ones make of me their
    symbol of courage,
They shall always escape dangers,
So shall it be even with one of the little ones,
They shall cause their hands to be ever present upon the foe,
    as they travel the path of life, it has been said, in this
    house.

I suppose the average modern city-dweller sees in these sentiments of primitive religion merely the workings of the pathetic fallacy. Properly here are shifting lights from an old American world of ordered loyalties, which a hundred generations past our own forefathers of weald and down might also have understood. But with hard-bitten logic and under the sovereignty of our own destructive powers we have withdrawn from all democratic contact with the animate children of Mother Earth—except, perhaps, when a lonely man finds something unpurchasable in the companionship of a dog. Even those plants and animals which are necessary to our well-being are no longer the recipients of our gratitude. Our religious sentiment outlaws them as it outlaws the sun and rain. Nature and all its works are merely materials to be taken, wasted and destroyed without responsibility to the past or to the future. But let us not make the mistake of thinking that the throwing off of natural bonds has been an act of wisdom or of intellectual freedom, for today we make a less worthy obeisance to our own inanimate machines, setting up a thousand nervous gods of speed and death and a thousand fleshy gods of comfort and decay. Have these things given a truer purpose to our lives and a finer inward happiness?

Under the inspiration of religion, albeit pagan, the makers of ceremonies, as Emerson says, "built better than they knew." One finds passages of great beauty in the rituals of the Redman. In the Osage Rite of the Chiefs there are descriptive touches such as the following[26]:

> In the fourth valley
> He beheld seven bends of a great river
> Enwrapped in a cloud of white smoke from many fires.
> Seven villages he saw among the seven bends of the river
> Enwrapped in a cloud of white smoke from many fires.

But are not ceremonial vestments embroidered and sacred altars enriched?

TRIAL BY POETRY

In the Far North enemies engage in poetic duels and intone their pleas for the public ear to the beat of the Arctic tambourine. Here nith songs, also called juridical songs and drum-contest songs, take the place of courts of law, the two contestants having it out with each other in a rival display of argument and vituperation. Undoubtedly the Eskimo in general get much pleasure in listening to these contests and the contestants themselves are not moved by bitter feelings alone. The airing of grievances and the gaining of public sympathy were undoubtedly the original purposes of the drum-contests but the theatrical opportunities were too great not to be seized upon. Drum-contest songs are still in use from Eastern Greenland to Western Alaska and their influence continues well down the Pacific coast.

Something of the yearning to excel in this strange practise is expressed in the following verses which tell how a man on shore sees a stranger on the sea and desires him as a drum-contest opponent[27].

Again, it seems that he down there will come ashore,
That that great kaiak down there will come ashore.
Will he not come this way, too, he down there,
One from another place than ours, will he not come here?
What a surprise! I can not forbear looking at him.
Will he not come this way, he down there, who does not
    belong here?
It's as if he down there is suspicious and wary of one,
How often has he down there sung drum-fight songs?
How many opponents in the drum-fight has he had?
What if he also made me one of his opponents!

An old pair of juridical songs concerns antagonists by
the names of Pulangit-Sissok and Savdlat, who rail at
each other in the approved fashion. The text was col-
lected by Rink in the late '60's but the first half of the
dialogue was recovered by Thalbitzer some 80 years
later in a somewhat softened form[28].

Savdlat speaks:
The South shore, O yes, the South shore I know it;
Once I lived there and met Pulangit-Sissok,
A fat fellow who lived on halibut, O yes, I know him.
Those South-shore folks can't talk;
They don't know how to pronounce our language;
Truly they are dull fellows;
They don't even talk alike;
Some have one accent, some another;
Nobody can understand them;
They can scarcely understand each other.

Pulangit-Sissok speaks:
O yes, Savdlat and I are old acquaintances;
He wished me extremely well at times;
Once I know he wished I was the best boatman on the
    shore;
It was a rough day and I in mercy took his boat in tow;
Ha! ha! Savdlat, thou didst cry most pitiful;
Thou wast awfully afeared;
In truth, thou wast nearly upset;
And hadst to keep hold of my boat strings,
And give my part of thy load.
O yes, Savdlat and I are old acquaintances.

The drum contest songs were used by both men and

women and the next example shows one woman paying her respects to another. It seems that the "poor Saatina" could not sing but was efficient enough at playing the tom-boy[29].

> I recognized the poor Saatina
> Who could not sing.
> I recognized the poor Saatina
> Who could not make drum songs.
> No, she was not such a one.
> A right merry person,
> A bright woman,
> Who always sang on the island Aaluib,
> Who always squalled with all her might.

It was doubtless through the training received in drum-contest songs that the Eskimo reached their rather exceptional ability at expressing moods. Also the Eskimo lack the intensively developed ceremonialism of American Indians in general, although possessing its rudiments, and they live close to hard realities. Take for instance the following piece which exhibits a quality of subjective insight rarely met with in primitive poetry[30].

> Great grief came over me—
> Great grief came over me,
> While on the fell above us I was picking berries.
> Great grief came over me
> My sun rose quickly over it.
> Great sorrow came over me.
> The sea out there off our settlement
> Was beautifully quiet—
> And the great, dear paddlers
> Were leaving out there—
> Great grief came over me
> While I was picking berries on the fell.

A much quoted poem exhibits a love of natural beauty apparently for itself alone. But there may have been in the author's mind an ulterior thought concerning seasonable weather[31].

I look toward the south, to great Mount Koonak,
To great Mount Koonak, there to the south;
I watch the clouds that gather round him;
I contemplate their shining brightness;
They spread abroad upon great Koonak;
They climb up his seaward flanks;
See how they shift and change;
Watch them there to the south;
How the one makes beautiful the other;
How they mount his southern slopes,
Hiding him from the stormy sea,
Each lending beauty to the other.

LOVE SONGS

While genuine love songs doubtless exist among some
Indian tribes, their importance has been over emphasized
in many articles dealing with Indian poetry. Indeed love
songs are most in evidence in those localities where the
Indian women have been exposed to make-and-break
contacts with whalers, fur-traders, buccaneers and what-
not. Thalbitzer has no divisions devoted to love songs
in his work on the poetry of the isolated Ammassalik
Eskimo, nor do they exist among the Yuma. In southern
Alaska and British Columbia where fur-traders and
whalers began to congregate after the voyages of Cook
and Vancouver there are songs of stranded and forsaken
women, some in the jumbled words of the Chinook trade
jargon and others in the native languages. The so-called
love songs of the Northwest Coast which seem most
authentic fit into the pattern of the poetic duel ridiculing
persons who have inflicted harm and with their answers
are more like public quarrelling than expressions of
tender passion.

The following piece is translated from the Kwakiutl
by Franz Boas and is entitled a love song. It was sung
by a jilted man[32].

Oh, how, my lady-love, can my thoughts be conveyed to you,
    my lady-love, on account of your deed, my lady-love?

In vain, my lady-love, did I wish to advise you, my lady-love,
　　on account of your deed, my lady-love.
It is the object of laughter, my lady-love, it is the object
　　of laughter, your deed, my lady-love.
It is the object of contempt, my lady-love, it is the object
　　of contempt, your deed, my lady-love.
Oh, if poor me could go, my lady-love! How can I go to you,
　　my lady-love, on account of your deed, my lady-love?
Oh, if poor me could go, my lady-love, to make you happy,
　　my lady-love, on account of your deed, my lady-love!
Now, I will go, my lady-love, go to make you happy, my
　　lady-love, on account of your deed, my lady-love.
Farewell to you, my lady-love! Farewell, mistress on account
　　of your deed, my lady-love!

In another example a woman complains that her
lover goes to Japan to hunt for seals. Her plaint brings
a rejoinder from the man that he is returning post haste.
Then there is a third song by him showing him dis-
missed for all his pains. I give part of the song of
Menmenlequelas after Tsak Edek deserts him".

Ye yaa ye ya ha!
You are cruel to me, you are cruel to me, you are cruel to me,
　　my dear!
Ye yaa ye ya ha!
You are hard-hearted against me, you are hard-hearted
　　against me, my love!
Ye yaa ye ya ha!
You are surpassingly cruel, you are surpassingly cruel against
　　me, for whom you pined.
Ye yaa ye ya ha!
She pretends to be indifferent, not to love me, my true-love,
　　my dear.
Ye yaa ye ya ha!
Don't pretend too much that you are indifferent of the
　　love that I hold for you, my dear!
Ye yaa ye ya ha!
Else you may be too indifferent of the love that I hold for
　　you, my dear!
Ye yaa ye ya ha!
My dear, you are too indifferent of the love that I hold for
　　you, my dear!
Ye yaa ye ya ha!
My dear, you go too far, your good name is going down,
　　my dear!

Ye yaa ye ya ha!
Friends, it might be well if I took a new true-love, a dear one.
Ye yaa ye ya ha!
Friends, it might be well if I had a new one for whom to
pine, a dear one.
Ye yaa ye ya ha!
I wish she would hear my love-song when I cry to my new
love, my dear one!

Among the Ojibwa are found songs which can hardly
be called love songs in the ordinary sense since they are
magical formulae with a practical rather than a senti-
mental value. Frances Densmore gives four examples to
be used against the males, each song having its mnemon-
ic picture on birch bark[34].

I
What are you saying to me?
I was arrayed like the roses.
And as beautiful as they!

II
I can charm the man
He is completely fascinated by me!

III
I can make that man bashful.
I wonder what can be the matter
That he is bashful?

IV
In the center of the earth
Wherever he may be
Or under the earth!

There are, however, real love songs among the
Ojibwa. These songs, according to Miss Densmore,
"mark a distinct phase in the development of music as a
means of expression." The words frequently run through
the entire song with little repetition and may be im-
promptu in their exact form. The Ojibwa sing their love
songs with a nasal twang which also characterizes the

songs of the scalp dance although this similarity may be fortuitous. Some of them are known to be old and may be sung with slight changes by either men or women. Here is a good example[35]:

> Although he said it
> Still
> I am filled with longing
> When I think of him.

Schoolcroft gives us an Ojibwa love song of a hundred years ago, which whether strictly aboriginal or not, does have the iterative Indian style[36].

> I will walk into somebody's dwelling,
> Into somebody's dwelling will I walk.
> To thy dwelling, my dearly beloved,
> Some night will I walk, will I walk.
> Some night in the winter, my beloved
> To thy dwelling will I walk, will I walk.
> This very night, my beloved,
> To thy dwelling will I walk, will I walk.

Love songs, except those which are supposed to have a magical and coercive quality of gaining affections and which might better be called love medicine, are not common among the tribes of the Great Plains. Nor are such songs listed by Ruth Bunzel among the kinds in use at Zuñi. The Tewa have them and I secured several examples in the forms of soliloquy and colloquy. While these are clearly enough of Indian composition, I believe the ultimate inspiration to have been Spanish. The same may be said of numerous pieces in Mexico and Guatemala.

European influence of a still different sort has been noted on the Mosquito Indians of Nicaragua. Cape Gracios á Dios and the hidden lagoons on either hand were long the haunt of pirates and buccaneers, and I fancy these cutthroats might, in their softer moments, have been sentimental enough. At any rate, in the middle of the last century the natives of this adventurous shore had love songs, several of which were written down by English residents. At the present time such songs are rare for in several journeys to eastern Nicaragua I could not secure a single example.

A fine piece, with original text and translation, is found in Charles Napier Bell's *Tangweera*[37]. He explains that "the young men and women are melancholy, and it is singular that all their music is melancholy. Cheerful music is quite beyond them. Their love songs are plaintive and sad, always the same tune and time, but the words are extemporized by them with a facility which to us would be almost impossible."

I

My girl, some days as you walk with your companions,
When the mist settles over the river mouth,
And the smell of the pitch-pine woods comes from the land,
Will you think of me and say:
"My lad have you really gone away?
Alas! my lad have I seen the last of you?
Shall I really never hear your voice again?
        Alas! Alas! Alas!"

II

My girl I am very sad for you,
I remember the smell of your skin.
I want to lay my head on your lap,
But here I am lying under a tree.
In my ear I only hear the noise of the sea
The surf is rising in the offing;
But I cannot hear your voice.
        Alas! Alas! Alas!

The Mosquito Indians were at the time of Columbus' Fourth voyage about the most uncivilized people in Central America. Originally from the wooded lowlands of South America they still have ceremonies which point to their first home.

The Tupi, of the lower Amazon and the coast of Brazil, have long had a reputation for poetic compositions especially among the French. This may date from 1550 when a large band of Tupi Indians took part in a festival at Rouen. In 1557 Jean de Lery recorded during voyage in Brazil several fragments of songs which had impressed him deeply. Much later the eminent Montaigne was provided with a few examples of Tupi songs by a man who had spent several years among these Indians, and was moved to declare that the verses were worthy of Anacreon.

Couto de Magalhães publishes the text and translation of two Tupi songs which are clearly love charms. One is addressed to Ruda who figures in the myths of the Tupi as a warrior residing in the clouds. He creates an amorous melancholy in the hearts of men, making them return home from long canoe trips. The song is translatable about as follows[38]:

> O Ruda, O Ruda,
> Thou who art in the skies
> And who lovest the rains,
> Make it so that he,
> No matter how many women he has
> Will think them all ugly.
> Make him remember me
> This afternoon
> When the sun gets in the west.

Another song, addressed to the Moon, also must be regarded as a magical prayer rather than a mere outpouring of emotion. It takes this form:

> New Moon, Oh, New Moon
> Remind that man of me!
> Here am I in your presence;
> Cause it to be that only I
> Shall occupy his heart.

The Brazilian ethnologist of half a century ago was quick to realize that many pieces in the Tupi language were nevertheless inspired by Portuguese models. He went so far as to demonstrate how, even in these second-hand compositions, there was a definite deterioration. Portuguese words replaced Indian ones until, finally, only a few meaningless syllables of the original Indian phrases were retained as a refrain. He might have gone farther and shown, how, in the breakdown of the truly Indian mode, magical prayers are replaced by sentimental praises.

DEATH AND ITS MYSTERY

Not all Indian songs about death are mourning songs; perhaps the most remarkable and beautiful ones are songs in which the dead reappear in dreams. Mourning songs are common enough among some tribes while among others they are eliminated by the taboo which forbids mention of a dead person's name. When permissible they have a somewhat broader appeal than love songs. The latter are, or should be, a private matter between two lovers while the former are a family or clan matter which often touches the entire community. The theme of communal loss is struck in the beginning lines of a Tlingit dirge[39]:

> The nation's canoe is drifting ashore with him
> My uncle is already dead . . .

Another one, following Swanton's text, deals with the all-encompassing mystery[40]:

> I always think within myself
> There is no place where people do not die.
> I do not know where my uncle is:
> Down into the spirits' cave around the world
> The spirits threw my uncle.

More poignant and less philosophical are the ending lines of a woman's song about her drowned brother[41]:

> Perhaps he went into the sun's trail
> So that I can never see him again.

I quote a mourning song of the Kwakiutl relating to a certain Moda'ena, member of the Cannibal Society, who was drowned with his sister. It was sung at his house by all the people of his village[42].

> *Ye he he ya!*
> It deprived me of my mind when the moon went down at the edge of the waters.
> *Ye he he ya!*
> *Ye he he ya!*
> It deprived me of my breath when the mouse-dancer began to gnaw on the water.
> *Ye he he ya!*
> *Ye he he ya!*
> It deprived me of my mind when Moda'ena began to utter the cannibal-cry on the water.
> *Ye he he ya!*

From the icy shores of Greenland comes an Eskimo song, translated by Thalbitzer, which voices the pretense that death is a new thing and not so bad at that[43].

> People have begun a new custom.
> People die now at intervals,
> Chopping out the little step,
> People die at intervals,
> After they have stepped through their heavy troubles.

The Papago believe that the dead return in dreams and teach curing songs. Many spiritualistic pieces are accredited to definite individuals and it is said that the dreams in which the songs were received usually took place immediately after death although in some cases months or even years elapsed before the spirit of the dead person returned to deliver his vital message. Some of the most striking songs seem to picture the last thoughts or, more daringly still, the flight of the soul. I give several examples in the fine renderings of Frances Densmore[44].

> In the great night my heart will go out,
> Towards me the darkness comes rattling,
> In the great night my heart will go out.
>
>   *   *   *   *   *
>
> A low range of mountains, towards them I am running
> From the top of these mountains I will see the dawn.
>
>   *   *   *   *   *
>
> I am dead here, I die and lie here,
> I am dead here, I die and lie here
> Over the top of Vihunput I had my dawn.

One gathers that elegies were common in ancient Mexico and in ancient Peru as well. This is natural enough in regions where aristocracy was recognized.

VOCATIONAL SONGS

Purely vocational songs are relatively unimportant in American Indian poetry partly because nearly every vocation is drawn into the ceremonial or religious field. There are paddling songs in the Far North while in New Mexico and Arizona men often sing to the scraping of hand stones while the women grind corn. More widespread still are gambling songs. Washington Matthews gives some of the songs used in connection with the moccasin game of the Navaho, played at night in the winter time. There are many animal songs, mostly derisive in character, the following ground squirrel song being typical[45].

> The squirrel in his shirt stands up there,
> The squirrel in his shirt stands up there;
> Slender, he stands up there; striped he stands up there.

The playing is terminated at the first streak of day
when the magpie song is sung[46].

> The magpie! The magpie! Here underneath
> In the white of his wings on the footsteps of morning.
> It dawns! It dawns!

Perhaps under vocational songs it would be well to
place the curing songs of medicine men. Most of these
are dream songs, however, or follow the pattern of
songs used in magic.

SONGS OF SEQUENCE

Songs of sequence is a term applied to sets of songs
dealing with the same theme and following each other
in a definite traditional order. Long ceremonies having
such songs are especially developed in the Southwest
whence the idea seems to have spread rather widely over
the Plains and into some parts of California but without
the same richness of detail as in the place of origin.
The Mountain Chant of the Navaho has thirteen sets
comprising 161 songs, the greatest number in a sequence
being 26 and the lowest seven. Says Washington
Matthews[47]:

> But how does the shaman remember the order of these
> songs of sequence? Does he possess any mnemonic key?
> He does. There is a myth for each set of songs, and this
> myth is the key. The song myths of this tribe are very
> numerous, and few songs except extemporaneous composi-
> tions, exist independently of a myth. In some instances the
> myth is the more important part of the work, and we are
> impressed with the idea that the myth maker composed
> his story first, and introduced his songs afterwards as em-
> bellishments; but in more cases the myth is a trifling element,
> and seems devised merely as an aid to the memory or as a
> means of explaining or giving interest to the songs.

I give an example from the myth of the Mountain
Chant of the Navahos to show the relation of prose and
poetry[48]:

The clouds hung over the mountain, the showers of rain fell down its sides, and all the country looked beautiful. And he said to the land "Aqalàni!" (greeting) and a feeling of loneliness and homesickness swept over him, and he wept and sang this song:

> That flowing water! That flowing water!
> My mind wanders across it.
> That broad water, that flowing water!
> My mind wanders across it.
> That old age water, that flowing water!
> My mind wanders across it.

The First and Twelfth Song of the Thunder in the Mountain Chant are translated by Matthews as follows[49]. They show an artful use of repetitions and parallel constructions.

First Song of the Thunder

I

> Thonah! Thonah!
> There is a voice above,
> The voice of the thunder.
> Within the dark cloud,
> Again and again it sounds,
> Thonah! Thonah!

II

> Thonah! Thonah!
> There is a voice below,
> The voice of the grasshopper.
> Among the plants,
> Again and again it sounds,
> Thonah! Thonah!

Twelfth Song of the Thunder

I

> The voice that beautifies the land!
> The voice above,
> The voice of the thunder
> Within the dark cloud
> Again and again it sounds,
> The voice that beautifies the land.

II

The voice that beautifies the land!
The voice below;
The voice of the grasshopper
Among the plants
Again and again it sounds,
The voice that beautifies the land.

The Night Chant by the same author is an even more monumental handling of the songs of sequence in a great curing ceremony of the Navaho. Here there are twenty four sequences with a total of 324 songs, strung like beads upon strings. Again we find the parallel constructions which seem to produce stanzas, as in the *Last Song in the Rock*[50].

I

At the Red Rock House it grows,
There the giant corn-plant grows,
With ears on either side it grows,
With its ruddy silk it grows,
Ripening in a day it grows,
Greatly multiplying grows.

II

At Blue Water House it grows,
There the giant squash-vine grows,
With fruit on either side it grows,
With its yellow blossom grows,
Ripening in one night it grows,
Greatly multiplying grows.

Next we have a song to Nayenezgani in two stanzas[51].

I

The Slayer of the Alien Gods,
That now am I.
The Bearer of the Sun
Arises with me,
Journeys with me,
Goes down with me,
Abides with me;
But sees me not.

II

The Child of the Water,
That now am I.
The Bearer of the Moon
Arises with me,
Journeys with me,
Goes down with me,
Abides with me;
But sees me not.

A second pair of poems to the same personage:

I

I am the Slayer of the Alien Gods.
Where'er I roam,
Before me
Forests white are strewn around.
The lightning scatters;
But 'tis I who cause it.

II

I am the Child of the Water.
Wher'er I roam,
Behind me
Waters white are strewn around,
The tempest scatters;
But 'tis I who cause it.

While a third concerns the bluebird[52]:

I

He has a voice, he has a voice.
Just at daylight Sialia calls.
The bluebird has a voice,
He has a voice, his voice melodious,
His voice melodious, that flows in gladness.
Sialia calls, Sialia calls.

II

He has a voice, he has a voice.
Just at twilight Sialia calls.
The bird tsolgali has a voice.
He has a voice, his voice melodious,
His voice melodious, that flows in gladness
Sialia calls, Sialia calls.

Also in this ceremony there are songs and prayers in which repetitions are made in accordance with colors, plants, and so forth, assigned to the four directions.

If the formal use of songs of sequence, as the first stage in ceremonial consolidations, extended across Mexico and down into South America no satisfactory evidence exists at the present time. F.P. and A.P. Penard report from Surinam that the Caribs have songs which are the *aula* or "word" of various spiritual beings. These may well belong in such a category. The word of the Snake Spirit they give in part[53]:

> I am the force of the spirit of the light-
>   ning eel, the thunder axe, the stone.
> I am the force of the fire fly; thunder
>   and lightning have I created.

The word of the Thunder they give entire:

> I am the thunder, the terror of the earth reflects my one-ness.
> The earth I do vibrate, I the Thunder.
> All flesh fears, that reflects the one-ness of the Thunder.
> I pass along my field.
> With swiftness all must clear the way.
> The lightning precedes me.
> The thunder-axe I have made, I the Thunder.

REVIVALIST VERSES OF THE GHOST DANCE RELIGION

The Ghost Dance Religion was a rather recent and most startling manifestation of Indian mass psychology, producing much fine poetry during the brief span of its existence as an organized cult. It was the united answer of the wilder tribes of the western states to alien aggressions which had destroyed the economies of Indian existence but had not yet completely broken the Indian morale. The new religion rested upon ancient fundamentals, upon ideas of coersive magic expressed in the forms of art. It attempted to reapply these ideas, as it were, to the violently new conditions of life. Perhaps it drew something from Christianity.

There were two cycles in the spread of the Ghost Dance Religion. The cult began either in western Nevada or eastern Washington about 1870 and the first expansion was towards the west. The originator of the movement is generally stated to have been a certain Tävibo, a minor chieftain of the Paiute tribe in the Walker Lake region, largely because he was the reputed father of Wovoka, hailed twenty years later as the Indian Messiah when the rejuvenated Ghost Dance was sweeping eastward over the Great Plains. But the evidence concerning the part that Smohalla, a medicine man living near Priest's Rapids on the Columbia River, played in the formation of the cult is more explicit and of earlier date than that of Tävibo.

The Indian office took notice of Smohalla in 1870, although the following clear statement of his beliefs is not so early[54]:

> They have a new and peculiar religion, by the doctrines of which they are taught that a new god is coming to their rescue; that all the Indians who have died heretofore, and who shall die hereafter, are to be resurrected; that as they will then be very numerous and powerful, they will be able to conquer the whites, recover their lands, and live as free and unrestrained as their fathers lived in olden times.

This was still the essence of the Ghost Dance Religion when it swept the Plains in 1890 but along the Columbia it was always referred to as the Dreamer Religion. The credo from the lips of Smohalla himself was taken down in 1884 by Major MacMurray who had been commissioned to persuade the Indians to take up homesteads and abandon their free life[55].

> You ask me to plow the ground! Shall I take a knife and tear my mother's bosom? Then when I die she will not take me to her bosom to rest.
> You ask me to dig for stone! Shall I dig under her skin for her bones? Then when I die I cannot enter her body to be born again.
> You ask me to cut my hay and sell it, and be rich like the white men! But how dare I cut off my mother's hair? . . .
> All the dead men will come to life again. Their spirits will return to their bodies again. We must wait here in the homes of our fathers and be ready to meet them in the bosom of our mother.

But Smohalla is said to have begun preaching "his peculiar theology" about 1850 and to have been instrumental in consolidating the western Shahaptin tribes in the Yakima war of 1855-56. If the story is true that he made a great pilgrimage down the Pacific coast to Mexico about 1860 and returned to his own people by way of Arizona and Nevada, he must, I think, be given the credit for spreading the seeds of the Ghost Dance Religion.

Both the first and second stages of the Ghost Dance Religion responded to a psychology of protest against an overwhelming material power. Smohalla's teachings were the result of aggressions which came thick and fast after the Nez Percé had extended an invitation to Spaulding, Whitman and their fellow zealots to preach at Lapwai and other missions. For other white men came to trade, to settle and to seek gold. The Modoc War of 1873-74 and the Nez Percé war of 1877 were the result of wrongs and coercions by the whites but perhaps the Indians found spiritual aid in their new religion.

Unfortunately there is a dearth of recorded songs of an early Ghost Dance type unless we imagine that unmodified Guardian Spirit songs were in use. If Kroeber is correct in stating that the first spread of the cult into California in the early '70's gave immunity against its second spread in the late '80's then the following piece from the Yokuts may be old, although I suspect it really belongs to the second epoch. The song was received in a dream by a shaman named Mayemai from his father[56]:

> Listen to me
> Mayemai!
> There in the east
> I shall emerge
> Twirling
> My hand feathers.

The second stage began with revelation of Wovoka when he was ill with fever during an eclipse of the sun. "When the sun died," he said, "I went up to heaven and saw God and all the people who had died a long time ago." He was hailed as a Messiah largely because the economic condition of all the tribes who had lived on the buffalo was then desperate.

The destruction of the great buffalo herds—millions of valuable food animals being slaughtered for petty profit on their hides alone within the space of four years (1880-84) by the whites—illustrates how inevitable was the clash between two philosophical systems of man's relation to nature. The Indian has ever abjured the waste of natural bounty and his religion has sought to give thanks for this bounty and at the same time assure its continuance. The white man's civilization, on the other hand, has most unwisely subordinated the conservation of public wealth to the acquisition of private wealth. A rapid exploitation and liquidation of natural resources in all parts of the world is now being carried on by the dominant white nations threatening the exhaustion of many materials. But if the Indian idea that nature is benevolent be a naïve untruth then the white man's idea that nature is inexhaustible is just as naïvely untrue and much more menacing to the future welfare of mankind.

The Ghost Dance Religion in its second phase spread out from the Paiute tribe and the earliest and simplest songs must therefore be sought there. Mooney, in preparing for his sympathetic study of the Ghost Dance, was able to secure but nine Paiute songs. Reduced to their briefest statements these sacred pieces are but two lines long. Always there are repetitions, however, which enlarge this briefest length. The first song refers to the open dance place in the dead of winter with the stars overhead. The Milky Way among American Indian tribes is the Spirit Road or the Pathway of Dead Warriors[57].

> The snow lies there, *ro-ra-ni!*
> The snow lies there, *ro-ra-ni!*
> The snow lies there, *ro-ra-ni!*
> The snow lies there, *ro-ra-ni!*
> The Milky Way lies there.
> The Milky Way lies there.

Then come simple invocations to elemental forces. In one song the line "the wind stirs the willows" is repeated thrice and "the wind stirs the grasses" is also repeated thrice. Another invocation goes:

> Fog! Fog!
> Lightning! Lightning!
> Whirlwind! Whirlwind!

The change is coming like a great storm and is pictured by the simplest but most powerful words, the songs rising to a climax.

> The whirlwind! The whirlwind!
> The whirlwind! The whirlwind!
> The snowy earth comes gliding,
> The snowy earth comes gliding,
> The snowy earth comes gliding,
> The snowy earth comes gliding.

> There is dust from the whirlwind,
> There is dust from the whirlwind,
> There is dust from the whirlwind,
> The whirlwind on the mountain,
> The whirlwind on the mountain,
> The whirlwind on the mountain.
>
> The rocks are ringing,
> The rocks are ringing,
> The rocks are ringing.
> They are ringing in the mountains,
> They are ringing in the mountains,
> They are ringing in the mountains.

Then, after the storm has passed, comes a picture of spring, implying the happy ending of the cataclysmic change.

> The cottonwoods are growing tall,
> The cottonwoods are growing tall,
> The cottonwoods are growing tall,
> They are growing tall and verdant,
> They are growing tall and verdant,
> They are growing tall and verdant.

Among other tribes who took the Ghost Dance ceremonial from the Paiute the songs are generally more elaborate. Repetition still serves to give a strange form to some of the songs, but as a rule one restatement is deemed sufficient. The subject matter becomes more specific with references to the Crow, the Eagle or Thunderbird, the Buffalo, etc., as well as to psychic experiences in meeting the dead.

Mooney gives 73 songs for the Arapaho tribe, most of them based on individual dreams and resembling the old time Guardian Spirit songs. But they often refer to encounters in the spirit world with dead friends at which games were played over and happy hunts were renewed. And there are some pieces which advance the argument in other ways. For instance, the following

song tells how the father will withdraw his favors from
the whites and give them again to his red children[58].

> My children, when at first I liked the whites,
> My children, when at first I liked the whites,
> I gave them fruits,
> I gave them fruits.

Or this piece which thrills with the joy of living.

> My children, my children,
> The wind makes my head feathers sing—
> The wind makes my head feathers sing—
> My children, my children.

Then there are sudden turns from ecstasy to pathos.

> Father, have pity on me,
> Father, have pity on me,
> I am crying for thirst,
> I am crying for thirst;
> All is gone—I have nothing to eat
> All is gone—I have nothing to eat.

Next to the end comes a song to the Morning Star.

> Father, the Morning Star!
> Father, the Morning Star!
> Look on us, we have danced until daylight,
> Look on us, we have danced until daylight.
> Take pity on us—*Hi-i-i!*
> Take pity on us—*Hi-i-i!*

HISTORICAL POEMS APPROACH THE EPIC

Poems which deal with historical characters or events
were rather common in ancient America and some of
them approach the epic as giving extensive narratives
lighted by nationalistic ideals. For instance among our
northern Indians there are such pieces as the *Walum
Olum* or *Red Score* of the Delaware which presents his-
torical traditions reaching back several centuries and has

some passages of literary merit. Then there is the Iroquois *Book of Rites* which memorializes the Great League, a consolidation of related tribes following the breakdown of the Mound Builder civilization. This wide-spread calamity may have been brought about by the introduction of European epidemic diseases after the voyage of Columbus. The Great League rested on the teachings of Hiawatha for its ethical features while its legal form was evolved in council and over much opposition. The Book of Rites, composed long after the events, is essentially a recitation broken by occasional hymns and dirges.Perhaps the most notable is a summary which in poetic form is arranged as follows by Hale[59]:

> Woe! Woe!
> Hearken ye!
> We are diminished!
> Woe! Woe!
> The cleared land has become a thicket
> Woe! Woe!
> The clear places are deserted.
> Woe!
> They are in their graves—
> They who established it—
> Woe!
> The Great League,
> Yet they declared
> It should endure—
> The Great League
> Woe!
> Their work has grown old.
> Woe!
> Thus we are become miserable.

Probably the oldest fragments of New World literature are laments for the great Toltec captains of the twelfth and thirteenth centuries[60]. The best preserved hymn refers to the rise of the Toltec power in Yucatan and its fall in the valley of Mexico, corresponding to the winning of the Maya city of Chichen Itza by Nacxitl-

Quetzalcoatl in 1191 and the abandonment of Teotihua-
can by Matlaxochitl and other Toltec lords in 1220 A.D.

A Toltec Lament

Here begins the kettle-drum hymn
Tico, tico, toco, toto, and the hymn ends
With tiquiti, titi, to titi.

In Tollan, alas! stood the House of Beams,
Where still the serpent columns stand.
But Nacxitl, our noble lord, has departed,
He has gone into the far country.
(Already our lamented princes have departed!)
And there in the Red Land he is undone.

In Cholula we were when we set forth
For Poyautecatitlan to cross the water in boats:
The wept for ones have departed!

I have come to the foreign boundaries
I, Ihuiquecholli, I, Mamaliteuchtli:
I am sad for my lord Ihuitimalli is gone.
He deserts me, I who am Matlacxochitl.
Weep, weep! O, weep, weep, weep!

That the mountains tumbled, I wept
That the sea rose up in dust, I lamented,
Wailing that he, my lord, had gone.

In the Red Land, alas! thou art awaited
And there thou art bidden to sleep!
O only weep, weep!

Thou hast already set forth my lord lhuitimalli,
Xicalango-Zacanco has passed to thy command.
Alas and nevermore! Weep, weep!

Thy house will remain forever, thy palace
Carried across the sea will always stay.
Thou hast left Tollan of the boundaries
Desolate here, weep, ah weep!

Without ceasing that lord, that Timallo wept:
Thy house will remain forever.

Thou first didst paint the stone and wood in Tollan
There where thou camest to rule, Nacxitl our noble
   lord!
Never will thy name be forgotten,
Always will thy people mourn thee, bewail thee!

The Turquoise House, the Serpent House
Thou alone didst set it up in Tollan,
There where thou camest to rule, Nacxitl our noble
   Lord!

The Maya Prophecies of the Katuns contain some references to early times since they are arranged in cycles of 13 katuns of 7200 days each according to the idea that events repeat themselves. These prophecies are constructed in the form of chants. The Prophesy of Katun 9 Ahau, covering events from 1556 to 1575 belongs to the era of persecution under the Spanish Inquisition. History furnishes few more telling indictments directed at their conquerors by a conquered people than this outcry of the disillusioned Mayas. I make three slight changes in Roys' translation[61] of the latter part of this prophesy although aware that more extensive re-phrasing would emphasize the poetic character of the satirical statement.

> Then began the building of the church
> Here in the center of Tihoo:
> Great labor is the destiny of the katun.
> Then began the execution by hanging,
> And the fire at the ends of their hands.
> Then also came ropes and cords into the world.
> Then came the children of the younger brothers
> Under the hardship of legal summons and tribute.
> Tribute was introduced on a large scale,
> And Christianity was introduced on a large scale.
> Then the seven sacraments of God's word were
>   established.
> Receive your guests heartily; our elder brothers come!

No epics pure and simple have survived from ancient America but there are epic-like compositions. The Cakchiquels of Guatamala have an Odyssey which tells how people under valiant leaders set out from Tollan, overcoming natural and supernatural difficulties. Most of this tribal narrative displays a poetic imagery and some of it a distinctly poetic form. If this be history then it is history in a cosmogonic setting with heroes who bulk large in a twilight of the gods. An early passage is about as follows[62]:

And soon the divination began with them. A bird called the guard of the ravine began to complain within the gate of Tollan as we were going forth from Tollan.

"You shall die, you shall be lost, I am your portent," said this brute to us. "Do you not believe me? Truly your state shall be a sad one." Thus spake to us this brute as is related.

Then another bird called the owl, seated on a red tree, complained and said thus: "I am your portent," he said. "You are not our portent, although you would like to be." we answered this owl. Such were the messengers who gave them their idols said our fathers, our ancestors of old.

Then another bird called the parroquet complained in the sky and said: "I am your portent, you shall die." But we said to the brute, "Do not speak thus: you are but the sign of spring. You wail first when it is spring; when the rain ceases, you wail." Thus we spoke to him.

Even more remarkable is the Popul Vuh or Sacred Book of the Quiché tribe for here there is, as Alexander points out, "the element of critical consciousness, giving the flavor of philosophical reflection." The recital of Creation resembles that of the Bible, nevertheless we cannot be sure that it is not a pagan parallel.

The self-glorification motive is put to scorn in a passage of the Popul Vuh which relates the unkingly end of a certain Vukub-Cakix. He was perhaps a Toltec overlord who hoped to lead the Quiché to the light in a cultural sense[63].

I will be their sun, I will be their light, I will be the moon to illumine them . . .
For of silver are the balls of my eyes and their sockets are set with resplendent jade; my teeth shine like precious stones, like the clarity of heaven . . .
In this manner, then, I am the sun and the moon, the cause that civilizes and makes wise the sons and daughters of the land.
So spake Vukub-Cakix. But really he was not the sun, and it was only the pride of plumes and metallic glitterings that make him speak thus.

Next it is explained how two young heroes despoiled Vukub-Cakix of his glory by pulling his teeth!

No examples of pre-Columbian drama have come down to us, but there are references enough to plays and pageants. Father Coto says of the Cakchiquel: "They are friendly to making colloquies and speaking verses in their dramas." At Copan we find theater-like constructions and at Chichen Itza there are platforms upon which it is presumed dramas were enacted. Several post-Columbian plays after the European religious models have been reported in Central America while from eighteenth century Peru comes the famous drama of Ollanta. It shows no traces of pre-Spanish poetic style and seems to have been modelled directly upon a mediocre European work. While agreeing with Hills[64] that it has little intrinsic merit, I certainly cannot agree with him when he says "Ollanta is the most important literary work that has been composed in any language indigenous to America." Rather its European reception was a reflection of Victorian taste.

STYLE IN OLD AMERICAN LITERATURE

Hundreds of mutually unintelligible languages are spoken by natives of the New World and even if most of the consolidations suggested by scientific linguists hold true, there must remain fifty or more unrelated linguistic stocks. For practical purposes each strongly defined language is an independent analysis—the terms of which exist only in the group mind—of all the material facts, actions, mental states and social conventions in settings of time and space, of which the members of the group are conscious, and concerning which they wish to exchange communications.

Language, like any other social tool, refines itself

through use and takes on appreciated characters of ease and beauty. The deliberate application of the more precise and pleasing ways of communicating thought everywhere gives rise to high style and fine art. Style is so intimately involved in the organic possibilities of a particular language that it cannot, properly speaking, be translated except in so far as it concerns the sequence and arrangements of materials. It can be matched in general effect, and that is about all. In translating poetry, then, the thought and the emotional environment of the thought, can be restated but not the poetic style *per se*.

But, it seems that ideas, quite aside from the streams of sound which impart them, may have absolute distinction, crystalline simplicity and other gem qualities. Ideas can be looked upon as arrangements of thought stimuli and sometimes a single simile, which we call poetic, may hold a vital comparison or imagery capable of passing freely across the frontiers of speech. It is style of thought rather than style of words which principally concerns the translator.

Indeed, it is difficult enough even to define style in any particular language. Speaking of the esthetic character of Mohave myths Kroeber says in one place:[65]

> We are thus face to face with a style of literature which is as frankly decorative as a patterned textile. The pattern is far from random; but it is its color and intricacy, its fineness and splendor, that have meaning, not the action told by its figures.

In another place the same writer speaks more broadly[66]:

> For centuries hundreds of thousands of human beings have been forming a style, a variety of styles, according to

nation and occasion, in which they expressed some of their profoundest feelings; and we cannot make a single exact and intelligible remark about their accomplishments.

It is of course true that we cannot judge style in the Redman's use of words except in so far as it is discernible in concentration or picturesqueness of thought above the mill-run of ordinary speech and in unusual rhythmic effects and balanced logical constructions. Among the Tewa, for instance, the poetic style is much more concentrated than the colloquial one and it contains "high words" and ceremonial phrases. Sahagun complained that Aztec poems and religious chants were esoteric to a degree. "They were composed," he says, "with such deceit that they proclaim only what the demon demands." When, however, an Aztec poet uses such a phrase as "I, the singer, polished my noble, new song like shining jade" we may be assured that style had passed out of the stage of natural selections and into the stage of purposeful cultivation.

The device of rhyme seems not to have been used by the most cultivated Americans of pre-Columbian times, although some interesting uses of it are found in post-Columbian poems from Peru. Nor were there any certain stanza forms except such as were brought about by the repetition of phrases. The outstanding feature of American Indian verse construction comes from parallel phrasing, or, let us say, repetition with an increment, which gives an effect not of rhyming sounds but of rhyming thoughts. Sometimes the ceremonial pattern demands a repetition for each world direction with formal changes involving the color, plant, animal, and so forth, associated with each station on the circuit. But there are other manifestations of parallelism of a more subtle cast. For instance, the Osage ritualist threads the laby-

Drummer.

rinth of apparent fact to reach ultimate truth in the
Little House of Mystery in the following parallels[67]:

> Towards what shall they direct their footsteps as they
> travel the path of life? They said, as has been said, in this
> house.
>
> *It is toward four little valleys that they shall direct their
> footsteps as they travel the path of life.*
>
> Verily, it is not four little valleys that is meant.
> *It is towards four herds of animals that they shall direct their
> footsteps as they travel the path of life.*
>
> Verily, it is not four herds of animals that is meant.
> *It is the little house toward which they shall direct their
> footsteps as they travel the path of life!*

I have explained how poetry is racked upon musical
frames and how it develops artistically out of what sur-
vives with least mutilation from the bed of Procrustes.
While rhythm might conceivably arise as an absolute
esthetic invention, actually in American poetry it is
induced by drummings and other pulsations. "The
rhythmic sense of primitive people," says Franz Boas[68],
"is much more highly developed than our own." He
adds: "It requires careful study to understand the struc-
ture of primitive rhythm, more so in prose than in song
because in this case the help of the melodic pattern is
lacking." Here rhythm is conceived as a complex un-
dulation in spoken or chanted words which represents
ease and is capable of producing an effect of pleasure.
But I think a close analogy holds between the esthetics
of poetic diction superimposed on music and the esthetics
of decorative art superimposed on a textile fabric. In
both cases there is a regulating order which reveals the
certain road to beauty.

Many figures of speech and circumlocutions have
their origin in the uses of religion, and perhaps we might

say that the emotional enlargement of religious concepts gives the poet his first opportunity. Aztec ceremonies, grim and grisly with human sacrifice, albeit spectacular and dramatic to the last degree, gained little from the plastic art of the sculptor but much from the euphemistic phrasing of the singer. The latter was able to disclose the hidden spirituality and sincerity of acts, which judged out of their context, could only arouse the sensation of cruel horror.

Take, for example, the Aztec hymn to Xipe Totec, Lord of the Flayed, a foreign god who acquired a wide vogue among Mexican tribes. His ritual challenged all others in the sheer achievement of grewsomeness. But except for the opening passage the hymn addressed to this god deals with returning springtime and the green of corn fields which must be brought to maturity[69].

Song to Xipe Totec, Lord of the Flayed
Thou Night-toper, who so bashful?
Then don thy masquerade,
The golden raiment, put it on!

Let thy jade waters descend, my Lord:
To green plumes the cypress turns,
To green plumes the fire-snake turns,
And the season of hunger leaves me.

Perhaps I shall be stricken
Upon the ground, I, the young maize stem.
My heart is like jade but I would
It were golden. Joyous! when first
It is ripe and the war-chief born!

With a plenteous maize field, my Lord,
Thy worshipper looks to thy mountain
And thee! Joyous! when first
It is ripe and the war-chief born!

There are phrases here which may seem somewhat cryptic. The golden raiment is, of course, the skin of the flayed victim. In the second verse the fire serpent of the dry season changes to the feathered serpent of the rainy season.

More occult still is the hymn addressed to the Fire God of the Aztecs, here called the Yellow-faced One but also known as the Turquoise Lord.

Song of the Yellow-faced Ones

In Tzommolco, my fathers, shall I affront you?
In Tetemocan shall I affront you?

In the House of Music, oh my Lords, the yucca tree booms
In the House of Disguises the masquerade has come down.

In Tzommolco they have begun to sing;
In Tzommolco they have begun to sing.
Why come they not hither,
Why come they not hither?

In Tzommolco human beings shall be given,
The Sun has come up!
Human beings shall be given.

In Tzommolco now ceases the song,
Without effort he has grown rich, to lordship he has
    attained,
It is miraculous his being pardoned.

Oh, little woman utter the speech,
Lady of the House of Mist, utter the speech abroad!

His priests prepare a sacrifice to the Sun in Tzommol-co, a temple in the ward of the travelling merchants in ancient Mexico City (Tenochtitlan). In the House of Music the shell trumpets and the drums were kept: "the yucca tree booms" refers to the latter, for the hollow log drums of the Aztecs were commonly made of this wood. At the conclusion of the human sacrifice to the rising Sun the offerer of the ceremony receives his reward in wealth and honors. These the Sun has power to convey while a mountain goddess of the morning mist broadcasts his action.

Concentration of thought reached its peak in the monosyllabic language of the Mayas. The original text of the Maya chant printed below has 90 syllables, while Brinton's English rendering contains 118 syllables or thirty per-cent more[70]. But English is itself a speech which excels in brevity.

> Eat, eat, while there is bread,
> Drink, drink while there is water;
> A day comes when dust shall darken the air
> When a blight shall wither the land,
> When a cloud shall arise,
> When a mountain shall be lifted up,
> When a strong man shall seize the city,
> When ruin shall fall upon all things,
> When the tender leaf shall be destroyed,
> When eyes shall be closed in death;
> When there shall be three signs on a tree,
> Father, son and grandson hanging dead on the
>   same tree;
> When the battle flag shall be raised,
> And the people scattered abroad in the forest.

The one thing that remained to be developed in the poetic expression of the American Indian was the individual point of view. But perhaps the world is richer by reason of this lack which leaves the social mode uncompromised.

ON TRANSLATING INDIAN POETRY

It is perhaps inevitable that many translators of Indian poems should color, or discolor, primitive ideas with civilized conventions, and this without any intention to deceive. Often their renderings depart so widely from the original texts—as ethnologists know the sense of them—as to leave nothing that is validly Indian, especially when rhyme or warping verse forms are employed. It is well, therefore, to consider the translator's handicap, and also to establish standards of success.

First of all it must be admitted that some pieces are falsely called Indian, being actually nothing more than compositions by whites in what is fondly believed to be a savage mode. The Taensa songs perpetrated by Parisot in a fabricated language were an elaborate fraud but most writers of spurious Indian songs do not bother with native texts.

Longfellow's *Song of Hiawatha* is not itself a translation but it has affected translations. It is essentially a literary creation in a peculiar style which the public has come to accept as one befitting Indian materials. Longfellow had before him only Schoolcroft's stilted transcriptions of a few Indian myths. He did not know that Hiawatha flourished about 1600 A.D. and was one of the founders of the original League of the Iroquois. Also he wove into this poem, with its strange medley of mythological incidents mostly taken from the Ojibwa, a love theme which joined the Iroquois of New York with the Sioux of far-off Dakota. He patterned his verse form, with its effective iterations, on the Scandinavian Eddas. It is irony indeed, that Longfellow's Indian Edda—to use his own phrase—should be accepted as archetype not only of Indian expression but also of the Redman's sentiment.

Four great recorders of American Indian poetry have established standards by which the work of others may be judged. The first and greatest of these is Bernardino de Sahagun, conservator of the soul of ancient Mexico. This Spanish priest arrived in Tlaltelolco in 1529, only eight years after Cortes had taken the nearby capital of the Aztecs. He devoted a long life to compiling information on the pre-Spanish culture. The second is Dr. Washington Matthews who served for many years as a physician on the Navaho Reservation. His lasting monuments are *The Mountain Chant* and *The Night Chant*. The third is Francis La Flesche, himself an Indian of the Omaha tribe and the best student of his race. During the last years of his life La Flesche freed himself from earlier subordinating influences and achieved a great triumph in recording and translating the sacred chants of the Osage tribe. The fourth most eminent achievement in the field of primitive American poetry is that of William Thalbitzer for his thorough study of the songs of the Ammassalik Eskimo. Although a Dane he exhibits remarkable felicity of expression in putting Eskimo over into English.

Sahagun recorded the Mexican songs in the Mexican language and in the same tongue he added glosses to explain symbolic passages in everyday words. He did not make translations of these pieces into Spanish, which is fortunate, for had he done so it is highly probable that his manuscript would have been destroyed. As it was no publication of this or any other part of his splendid compilation was permitted during his lifetime for fear that it would keep alive pagan beliefs and practices which the church was trying to stamp out. The manuscripts lay unnoticed until the end of the eighteenth century. The part containing the ancient songs was first translated into English by Brinton under the title of *Rig Veda Americanus*. A better translation has been made into German by Seler but it seems that there are archaic expressions which even Sahagun could not explain in his glosses.

The other writers whose works are to be commended from the double standard of fidelity to the original sources and artistic quality in the rendering belong to the school of modern ethnology. They preserve a golden mean while many other moderns incline to one of two extreme: some give prosaic renderings of poetic texts and some give poetic renderings which wander so far from originals that they no longer serve as true indices of Indian mentality. After all translation is the carrying over of the totality of expressed thought from the terms of one language to the terms of another.

There is over translation and under translation. Let us consider examples of each for the purpose of defining somewhat more precisely the personal equation of the translator. The Hako Ceremony of the Pawnee possesses dignity and poetic quality of high order and its interpretation with all covert meanings was an achievement of Alice Cunningham Fletcher at the turn of the century. She was assisted by James R. Murie as interpreter and Tabirussawitchi, an elder of the Pawnee tribe, as interpreter. The songs were recorded by phonograph and transcribed into scale music. This Hako Ceremony was an elaborate prayer for children and the welfare of the tribe expressed in symbolical language and action. The fertility of the earth responding to sun and rain produces human food and human happiness. The Corn Mother is the intermediary between man and the cosmic powers.

Admitted that more is meant than the language conveys, nevertheless it is perhaps unfortunate that the English words used by Miss Fletcher in her "rhythmic renditions" go so far beyond the Pawnee words. Implications in regalia, in ceremonial objects and in the pantomime of dancers may form a running commentary in an Indian ceremony and may have esoteric significance in accordance with a veritable philosophy of illusion. But is it wise to enrich the actual text in such fashion as to bring out the context?

Let me illustrate with the first stanza of a typical song as translated by Miss Fletcher[71]:

> Tiráwa harken! mighty one,
> Above us in blue silent sky!
> We standing wait thy bidding here.
> The Mother Corn standing waits,
> Waits to serve thee here;
> The Mother Corn stands waiting here.

The Pawnee text out of which this stanza is constructed
is mostly a repetition of the simple phrase,

> Mother, now I standing, hold.

How then did Miss Fletcher obtain her opening
address to the supreme deity of the Pawnee and her
varied renderings of the other lines? Well the Corn
Mother is an object held in the hand of the performer
consisting of an ear of corn fastened to a stick with a
plume at the top and with the uppermost kernels painted
blue. The ear is therefore a combination of supernatural
powers in earth below and heaven above, since blue is
the color of the sky. The feather is a cloud or perhaps
Tirawa. Also, according to Miss Fletcher, the symbolism
is continued in the bowl of sacred blue paint. There is,
I suppose, no reason for doubting that the ceremony as a
whole is addressed to Tirawa. Nevertheless the re-
assemblage of these intimations into the specific phrase:

> Tiráwa hearken! mighty one
> Above us in blue silent sky!

seems to me to go far beyond the proper rights of trans-
lation. The expansion found in this poem is characteris-
tic of the method used for the entire ceremony with its
twenty rituals.

But under translation is also found. For instance,
Frank Russell's translations of Pima songs are a sort of
blanc mange which do not do justice to the material.

Take the Wind Song which he translates as follows in one of his better renderings[72]:

> Wind now commences to sing;
> Wind now commences to sing.
> The land stretches before me,
> Before me stretches away.
>
> Wind's house now is thundering;
> Wind's house now is thundering;
> I go roaring o'er the land
> The land covered with thunder.
>
> Over the windy mountains;
> Over the windy mountains,
> Came the myriad legged wind;
> The wind came running hither.
>
> The Black Snake Wind came to me;
> The Black Snake Wind came to me
> Came and wrapped itself about
> Came here running with its song.

On the basis of the interlinear words the following is a closer and certainly more interesting rendering of this piece.

> Here the wind begins to sing.
> There before me stretches the land.
> Here the wind begins to sing.
> There before me stretches the land.
> Begins to sing,
> There before me stretches the land.
>
> Wind-house thunder! wind-house thunder!
> I go there in the thunder-covered land.
> Wind-house thunder! wind-house thunder!
> I go there in the thunder-covered land.
> Wind-house thunder!
> I go there in the thunder-covered land.
>
> Over windy mountain! Over windy mountain!
> Everywhere centipede gusts came running.
> Over windy mountain! Over windy mountain!
> Everywhere centipede gusts came running.
> Over windy mountain!
> Everywhere centipede gusts came running.

Black Snake Wind! Black Snake Wind!
Here came running in a song, tied up in a song.
Black Snake Wind! Black Snake Wind!
Here came running in a song, tied up in a song.
Black Snake Wind!
Here came running in a song, tied up in a song.

In their study of *American Indian Poetry* Eda Lou
Walton and T. T. Waterman go into a fuller examination
of the discrepancies between Russell's literal texts and
his literary renderings and also call attention to a
Navaho poem doubly translated by Mathews in the
Night Chant and by Goddard in *Navaho Myths, Prayers
and Songs*, as poetically very different. But Goddard was
able to give considerable distinction to the words of
Apache ceremonies where his work stands alone. The
short songs by Frances Densmore in her numerous papers
on American Indian music are often very fine as are those
of Thomas Mooney in his classical *Ghost Dance Religion*.
Ruth Bunzel must certainly be praised for her handling
of Zuñi material, where Frank Hamilton Cushing and
Matilda Coxe Stephenson had preceded her. William
Jones has treated the shamanistic material around the
Great Lakes in more delicate fashion than some other
writers. As a rule the professional linguists are prosaic:
it seems that they pay attention merely to structures
and to the denotation of words, neglecting the connota-
tion. It is the old story of botanists not seeing the
beauty of flowers.

TEWA POETRY AS A TYPICAL EXHIBIT

In the Southwest the social and spiritual entities of
ancient America have survived to our times but today
the more precious elements are rapidly disintegrating
under manifold contacts. The Navaho retain the tradi-
tions of a semi-nomadic life and the Pueblo tribes those

of sedentary life reaching back to the times of the Cliff Dwellers. The ceremonial and artistic life of Zuñi is better known than that of any other Pueblo group. The other Pueblo groups, including the Hopi villages, the Keres villages and the Tiwa and Tewa villages have been indifferently reported upon, mostly by persons whose ceilings—to use an aeronautic term—are low.

The Tewa constitute a linguistic division of the Tanoan stock and live in the five villages of Tesuque, Nambe, San Ildefonso, Santa Clara and San Juan in the Rio Grande valley north and northwest of Santa Fé. They have been in contact with the white man since the Coronado Expedition and continuously since 1598 when the Spaniards took up residence across the river from San Juan of the Gentlemen—except for the interval of the Pueblo Rebellion (1680-1694). The native culture, always accepting some ideas from the outside, nevertheless managed to intensify its own religious and social life. This was the case until the era of railroad communication when an influx of the whites brought disease and economic pressure. Despoiled of much of their land and water, and burdened with tuberculosis and tracoma, the dwindling villages reached a low level about 1910. Since then there has been some increase in population but the uses of money have struck at the most sacred institutions from the inside.

The examples of Tewa poetry presented in this volume were collected in the years 1909, '10, '11 and '12 while I was engaged in ethnological field work for the American Museum of Natural History. The songs were taken down in native texts, with inter-linear translations and then converted into direct and simple English". Fortunately the Tewa language presents no unusual difficulties in translation.

While this collection does not by any means exhaust the repertory of the Tewa, it does, I believe, furnish examples of all types of poetic expression in use by them. As regards the secular and esoteric poems the reader will find material for comparison in the recent study of Ruth Bunzel entitled *Introduction to Zuñi Ceremonialism*. There are other publications which might be mentioned but space does not permit. I close with an invocation to the Makers of Storms recorded at Zuñi[74].

> Cover my earth mother four times with many flowers.
> Let the heavens be covered with the banked-up clouds.
> Let the earth be covered with fog; cover the earth
> with rains.
> Great waters, rains, cover the earth. Lightning cover
> the earth.
> Let thunder be heard over the earth, let thunder be
> heard;
> Let thunder be heard over the six regions of the earth.

Brooklyn Museum
    September 18, 1933.

Part I

HOME SONGS

· I ·

THE ROAD OF MAGIC

Yonder on White Mountain Plain
It was good in the long ago!
San Juan girls and San Juan boys,
Together they used to walk
Where lies the Road of Magic.

Yonder on Cactus Stalk Plain
It was good in the long ago!
Together we used to walk,
San Juan girls and San Juan boys,
Where lies the Road of Magic.

Yonder on Painted Mountain Plain
It was good in the long ago!
San Juan girls and San Juan boys,
With them I used to walk
Where lies the Road of Magic.

Here on Medicine Hill Plain
Again we walk together!
San Juan girls and San Juan boys,
Again we walk together
Where lies the Road of Magic!

· II ·

THAT MOUNTAIN FAR AWAY

My home over there, my home over there,
My home over there, now I remember it!
And when I see that mountain far away
Why, then I weep. Alas! what can I do?
What can I do? Alas! what can I do?
My home over there, now I remember it.

· III ·

I WONDER HOW MY HOME IS

In San Juan I wonder how my home is.
Surrounded by green cottonwoods my home is,
Now I remember all and now I sing!
Now I remember how I used to live
And how I used to walk amid my corn
And through my fields. Alas! what can I do?

· IV ·

THE WILLOWS BY THE WATER SIDE

My little breath, under the willows by the water side
    we used to sit
And there the yellow cottonwood bird came and sang.
That I remember and therefore I weep.
Under the growing corn we used to sit,
And there the little leaf bird came and sang.
That I remember and therefore I weep.
There on the meadow of yellow flowers we used to walk
Oh, my little breath! Oh, my little heart!
There on the meadow of blue flowers we used to walk.
Alas! how long ago that we two walked in that pleasant
    way.
Then everything was happy, but, alas! how long ago.
There on the meadow of crimson flowers we used to
    walk.
Oh, my little breath, now I go there alone in sorrow.

· V ·

BANTER

Oh, somewhere yonder in the west
You go away to gather wood.
And now you shout and now you sing.
Oh yes, I remember! Abruptly you left me!
Laughing was I, nevertheless, you left me!

· VI ·

LOST LOVE

At Su k'wa k'e there used to bloom a flower—
That flower, that flower, whene'er I see it now
Alas, so far away, why then I weep;
That flower, that flower, whene'er I see it now,
For yellow, fresh and full-blown once it bloomed.

· VII ·

THAMU'S SONG

Alas! this man of mine!
His words were like truth
When he talked to me.
His words were like truth,
But right away he proved
To be an arrant liar!

· VIII ·

SHADOWS

That somebody, my own special one,
Even his shadow and his voice are loved.
His foot fall even! But what can I do?
That other one, O how I hate his shadow!
His shirt is fine and white, his hat is gray,
His leggings and his shoes are beaded bright,
His neckerchief is gay and yellow—but
For all his clothes, his face, his face is black!

· IX ·

THE INCONSTANT LOVER

He speaks
Oh, Little Blue, at your door I wish to be,
At your door that once was blue and open wide,
But now is closed. At your door, I wish to be
Oh, my little breath! Oh, my little heart!

She speaks
To Comanche girls you paid those words, those eyes!
Your wish concerns me not and I can't be blamed
For that! It was under guns that you dared to pay!

· X ·

DISILLUSION

Long ago how fine was everything!
Fat mutton was all I ate,
Coffee and sugar were all I ate,
But now all I eat is the whip!

· XI ·

REGRET AND REFUSAL

The boy speaks
>All round about the door of your house
>The red and full blown flowers grow
>And there are striped ones of yellow
>And there are striped ones of white!
>
>About your door how gay it used to be,
>My little pony, even he had flowers,
>Alas, alas, and woe is me!

The girl speaks
>Once at my house how yellow, fresh
>And full blown was the flower you had!
>How green and fresh and full-blown
>Was the flower that once you had!

The boy speaks
>My woman also she has many flowers
>Yonder in Truchas, yonder in Seha.

The girl speaks
>So now he comes back to his sweetheart.
>So now you remember me and come back!
>Yes, yonder you thought again of your sweet-
>   heart
>For they sang you a song of corn grinding,
>Those young men there, on Saturday afternoon!

The boy speaks
>Alone with myself and seeing you never
>What can I do, alas what will avail?
>Because you leave me now, you leave me,
>But ever when I think of you I weep.

The girl speaks
> My foolish one, you cannot hold me now:
> No more will I remember. It is done.

· XII ·

RAGS ARE ROYAL RAIMENT......

"That dirty one, that ragged one."
Thus do they deride us two.

But you, you have good fortune;
Yellow clothes, pink clothes, blue clothes.
These are the only kinds you wear!

But you not mind to be a mule!

· XIII ·

WHEN THE TRADING PARTY SETS OUT

The men speak:
> On the road to the north
> We go with our packs.
> And there we will shout
> And there we will sing!

The women speak:
> Many things you have to remember,
> So that is why you leave us!

· XIV ·

WHEN THE WAR PARTY SETS OUT

So we have bad luck
For we are men,
You have good luck now
For you are women!

To Navajo towns we go
Ready for war, Goodbye!

· XV ·

A CORN GRINDING SONG OF TESUQUE

There towards the north,
There the fog is lying,
There the fog is lying.
In the middle stands Blue Corn
Happily, prettily, she is singing
Ha-we-ra-na na-a-se

There towards the west
There the fog is lying,
There the fog is lying,
In the middle stands Yellow Corn
Happily, prettily, she is singing
Ha-we-ra-na na-a-se

There towards the south
There the fog is lying,
There the fog is lying,
In the middle stands Red Corn
Happily, prettily, she is singing
Ha-we-ra-na na-a-se

There towards the east
There the fog is lying,
There the fog is lying,
In the middle stands White Corn
Happily, prettily, she is singing
Ha-we-ra-na na-a-se

· XVI ·

THE BLUE FLOWER BASKET

The blue flower basket
On the top of heaven seems.
It gleams and all is done!
Agowaha ne-e-e
Esha ha' we rana
Ma-a-si

· XVII ·

THE RABBIT BY THE RIVER

There by the river runs a little rabbit.
Why did you not catch him?
Why did you not kill him?
We feel like doing just that!
Bent over like a little old man
Off he goes with a watermelon;
Bent over like a little old man
Off he goes with a muskmelon!

· XVIII ·

RAINS FOR THE HARVEST

Over there in your fields you have
Musk-melon flowers in the morning.
Over there in your fields you have
Corn-tassle flowers in the morning.

In your fields now the water bird sings
And here in your village the fogs
And the black clouds come massing.
They come here to see! They come here to see!
Mbe'e a-ha we-o-'e

· XIX ·

THE CLOUD-FLOWER LULLABY

In the north the cloud flower blossoms,
And now the lightning flashes,
And now the thunder clashes
And now the rain comes down!
A-a-aha, a-a-aha, my little one.

In the west the cloud flower blossoms,
And now the lightning flashes,
And now the thunder clashes,
And now the rain comes down!
A-a-aha, a-a-aha, my little one.

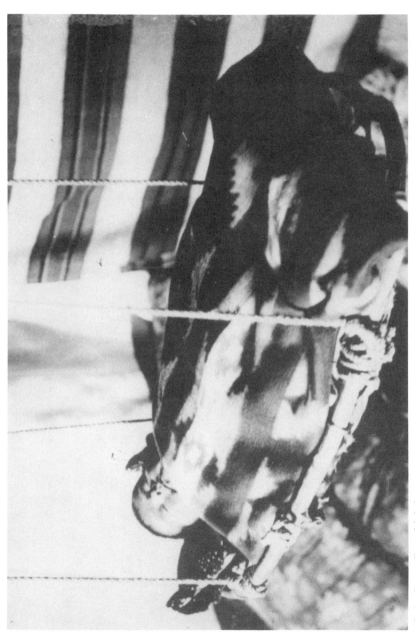

Baby in cradle, which is suspended from ceiling rafters.

In the south the cloud flower blossoms,
And now the lightning flashes,
And now the thunder clashes,
And now the rain comes down!
A-a-aha, a-a-aha, my little one.

In the east the cloud flower blossoms,
And now the lightning flashes,
And now the thunder clashes,
And now the rain comes down!
A-a-aha, a-a-aha, my little one.

· XX ·

A LULLABY OF NAMBE

Go to sleep,
Go to sleep,
Lest something come,
To take away
My little one.
So you must sleep,
My little one.

· XXI ·

LULLABY OF CANNIBAL GIANTS

Stop crying! Go to sleep, my little boy Primrose.
That Saveyo Sendo will take you if you cry.
Over there he will eat you, if you do not stop crying;
Right now he will eat you, if you do not stop crying.
That Saveyo Sendo in his bag he will put you.
Stop crying! Go to sleep, my little boy Primrose.
Over there he will take you, then I will be crying!
Very thick now are the leaves of the cottonwood,
Very thick now are the leaves of the willow,
There he will take you in under the willow,
That Saveyo Sendo whose teeth we all fear.
Over there now, if you do not stop crying,
Over there now, on the crest of the mountains,
Those Saveyo walk and they hear every sound.
And there in the mountains that one he will take you
Where now they are taking the big boys and girls.

· XXII ·

SLEEPY BIRD LULLABY

There are many sleepy little birds,
Sleepy little birds, sleepy little birds,
So go to sleep, my little girl,
My little Frosted-Cockle-Burr,
O, come you sleepy little birds
And slumber on her hollow eyes
That she may sleep the livelong day,
That she may sleep the livelong night.

· XXIII ·

CHILDREN'S FLOWER SONG OF NAMBE

Prettily we wear flowers.
Little flowers of the muskmelon we wear,
Little flowers of the watermelon we wear,
So now we wear flowers.

Kiva at San Ildefonso.

Part II

SACRED CHANTS AND CEREMONIAL SONGS

· XXIV ·

INITIATION CHANT OF THE KWIRANA K'OSA

Here and now we bring you, oh our old men gods,
Sun Fire Deity and Blue Cloud Person of the North,
Sun Fire Deity and Yellow Cloud Person of the West,
Sun Fire Deity and Red Cloud Person of the South,
Sun Fire Deity and White Cloud Person of the East,
Sun Fire Deity and Dark Cloud Person of the Below,
Sun Fire Deity and All-colored Cloud Person of the
      Above,
Here-at we bring you now your special prayer stick,
We make for you an offering of sacred meal,
A little bit for all, we make these offerings to you!

Stand ready, then, at dawn to walk
With rain upon the northward mountain top,
Upon the westward mountain top of the great lake dell,
Upon the southward mountain top where the Tshu
      people sit,
Upon the eastward mountain top of the great dawn,
Upon the mountain top that rests below the earth,
Upon the mountain top of the Sky Universe above!

Bring cloud flowers that are not barren of rain,
Set them upon the far off northward mountain top,
Set them thereat upon the westward mountain top,
Set them thereat upon the southward mountain top,
Set them thereat upon the eastward mountain top,
Set them thereat upon the mountain top below the
      Earth,
Set them thereat upon the mountain top above the Sky,
Thereat set them, those cloud flowers not barren of rain!

There on the middle mountains first lay fogs.
That is why from there to San Juan town ready at dawn
You bring your lightnings, thunders and your rains
    together,
Transforming with magic the fields that in the middle
    are!
And that is why the stretched-out plain is now revived,
And that is why the hills of the plain are now revived,
And that is why your shrinking lakes, your lakes
Where they are lying, are now revived thereat!

May all tame animals increase and children all,
For little people are we all to be loved of the Gods
As far away as our Great Mother's sound of breathing
Reaches. Even to the Utes, Apaches, Navajos,
Kiowas, Comanches, Cheyennes, even to all of them!
To the Mexican people, even to them it reaches!
To the people of America, even to them the sound
Of our Great Mother's breathing reaches. So now
They are loved of the Gods and each by the other loved!
So that is why we hope to find our living here,
We mortal men! Then place good summers and
Good days and nights of harvest! For each
The same, place then good days and nights of harvest!

· XXV ·

INITIATION SONG OF THE TEWA K'OSA

The K'osa make pantomime
    In Pine Tree Glade
    It rained this much
    In a water-hole amid the rocks.

The K'osa address Kâkanyu Sendo
    Old Man Kâkanyu!
    The big yellow eye
    Runs off in the water!

The K'osa make pantomime
    In Pine Tree Glade
    It rained this much
    In a water hole amid the rocks.

The K'osa address Uhu Sendo
    Old man Uhu!
    The big yellow eye
    Runs off in the water.

The Cloud People pursue the K'osa
    No, my man! No, my man.
    The yellow biscuit with a hole—
    That is all I mean!

· XXVI ·

LAKE SONG OF THE TEWA K'OSA

Towards Leaf Lake we are going
Under the farthest lightening we are going,
Under the thunder we are going,
Under the rain and the dew we are going,
Even now we are arriving.

· XXVII ·

HOW THE GODS ARE BROUGHT
A Dramatic Fragment

Argument: This is the culminating episode of a long
myth which tells how the two Little People, miracu-
lous twins, defeated the False Priests and established
the true rituals. They have been successful in earlier
tests but now comes the supreme test of bringing the
gods into the underground ceremonial lodge. The
ritual here described is used by the K'osa. They blow
ashes from the open hand to imitate a cloud and on
this cloud they see the rain gods walking.

The Twins hold dialogue
Then they two went to the fireplace, and out of it
took handfuls of ashes.
And standing where they were one said to the other:
"Yes, my twin, you go first, you try your magic
first!"
So that one threw the ashes in his hand towards
the north.
And he said: "Nothing at all I see there so next
your turn it is to make magic; and in what
direction do you mean, my twin?" he said.
"Well somewhere towards the east," that one said
deceitfully, but really towards the west he
threw his ashes. "Nothing at all I see
there, brother twin."

The False Priests make side remarks
Then the others said to one another. "From where
could those two bring something? Why do
they talk so uselessly?"

The Twins resume
"Yes, now you try it again, and in what direction,
my twin?"

"Well, somewhere over there," he said and made
ready to throw towards the north but
really towards the south he threw the
ashes. Then he said, "Nothing at all
appears, so next you try again."

The False Priests make side remarks
"What can those two bring from anywhere? Just
watch how they pretend! Pretty soon they
should be finished off!

The Twins resume
Again it is the older twin's turn. "Slowly now you
try it, my twin brother, but in what
direction?"
"Well, somewhere towards the west" and westward
he made like to throw the ashes, but
really to the east he threw them.
"Up yonder," he said, "up yonder at Stone Man
Lake the troubled waters go *tsha'amä!*
tsha'a mä! tsha'a mä!
"That is what I see and hear, so now quickly, my
twin; quickly, my twin; you must hurry!"
So next that one threw ashes, "But where," he said,
"but where?" and yonder towards Stone
Man Lake he likewise threw his ashes.
"Now, my twin, the water moves" he said,
"tsha'amä! tsha' amä! tsa' amä! You said
so, yes! but there in the middle of the lake
one is peeping out! I see him! From there
now they come out, they come out, they
come out around the edge of the lake! This
way and that they walk about!"

"From there now they lift up their fog rainbow and
to the north on Fish Ridge where the
ditch-head lies, they rest their fog rain-
bow. Now on the top of it they come to
that mountain where the ditch-head lies!
They come, my twin brother! So hurry,
twin brother!"

And next that one threw ashes towards Fish Ridge
where the ditch-head lies. "There they
come," he said. "From there they lift
their fog rainbow again and on Fish Sum-
mit they rest their fog rainbow! Now on
top of it they keep coming!"

"And now a cloud flower is seated there on Stone
Man Mountain top! Now it thunders hard!
a light gleams, the lightning flashes! And
now at Yunge village, the people are seeing
it. So now, my twin brother, you try it."

And next that one threw ashes towards Fish Summit
Lake. "There they have come, just as you
said. From there they lift up their fog
rainbow and at the town on the end of
Cedar Face they rest their fog rainbow.
Still on the top of it they keep coming!
And now it thunders strongly, hail and
great rain waters fall here at Yunge
village!

The False Priests make side remarks
Then the others said to one another, "What can
those two bring? Even now they should be
made what they will soon be made—
universe wanderers in the void!

Rattle-flower Youth and Flint-Corn youth speak
> Then Tini povi enu and Khu mbi enu said "Wait,
> all of you! Just wait, all of you!"

The Twins resume
> "Quickly, my twin," he said to him and threw
> ashes towards the town at the end of Cedar
> Face. "As you said, they come! From there
> next they lift their fog rainbow and
> towards Muddy Water Lake and there at
> Muddy Water Lake they rest their fog
> rainbow and on top of it they keep
> coming!"
> And more and more the lightning flashes entered
> the lodge where they were sitting as if
> destruction were coming. And now on the
> roof of the lodge the footsteps of the
> watchers sounded and they entered.
> "Next quickly, my twin brother! There as you said
> they come to Muddy Water Lake! and now
> they lift their fog rainbow to Blue Willow
> leaf Lake and rest."
> And then even the houses shook with thunder.

The False Priests make remarks
> And now those others looked at one another and
> spoke. "But what can those two bring?"
> And though they were seeing, still they
> were not believing.

Battle-flower Youth and Flint-Corn Youth speak
> "But wait a little! but wait! You will see what you
> will see," they said.

The Twins resume
>   "Then quickly" he told him, "my twin brother,
>   they have come to Blue Willow Leaf Lake,
>   as you say! From there now they lift up
>   their fog rainbow and here, where the
>   stone gods of Yunge live, they rest their
>   fog rainbow. Now they come on! Here
>   they come, now!"
>   So those two said. And the hail was thrown sud-
>   denly into the lodge.
>   And the White Corn Girls stood there with baskets
>   of meal ready to give an offering of food!
>   Then quickly he said to his twin brother: "Here
>   in Yunge where the Stone Gods live you
>   said they were coming. And now they lift
>   their fog rainbow right to the lodge. At
>   the head of the ladder now they put down
>   their fog rainbow. Here they come now!
>   Enter! Enter our Old Men Gods!
>   So now those false ones were walled in by the
> lightnings. They were struck by the lightnings and their
> entrails were riven.

· XXVIII ·

URU-TU-SENDO'S SONG

Yonder comes the dawn,
The universe grows green,
The road to the Underworld
Is open! yet now we live,
Upward going, upward going!

· XXIX ·

SONG OF THE SKY LOOM

Oh our Mother the Earth, oh our Father the Sky,
Your children are we, and with tired backs
We bring you the gifts that you love.
Then weave for us a garment of brightness;
May the warp be the white light of morning,
May the weft be the red light of evening,
May the fringes be the falling rain,
May the border be the standing rainbow.
Thus weave for us a garment of brightness
That we may walk fittingly where birds sing,
That we may walk fittingly where grass is green,
Oh our Mother the Earth, oh our Father the Sky!

· XXX ·

THE CORN-SILK-WOMEN'S SONG

Ones of the Northern Lake
Corn-Silk-Women ye are,
And now ye come to us!

Then lay long life at once upon us,
And upon our children
The love of all the gods!

May our children have many children
And our girls of San Juan live long!

And now we seek to hear
The Corn-Silk-Women say
Such words as we have said!

Long life now we ask,
And to be loved,
And to rear many children,
And to be given kindly fates!

· XXXI ·

RAIN MAGIC SONG

Ready we stand in San Juan town,
Oh, our Corn Maidens and our Corn Youths!
Oh, our Corn Mothers and our Corn Fathers!

Now we bring you misty water
And throw it different ways,
To the north, the west, the south, the east
To heaven above and the drinking earth below!

Then likewise throw you misty water
Toward San Juan!
Oh, many that you are, pour water
Over our Corn Maidens' ears!
On our Wheat Maidens
Thence throw you misty water,
All round about us here!

On Green Earth Woman's back
Now thrives our flesh and breath,
Now grows our strength of arm and leg,
Now takes form our children's food!

· XXXII ·

SONGS IN THE TURTLE DANCE OF NAMBE

First song
> Yellow Flower Girl!
> Blue Flower Girl!
> Mottled Corn Girl!
> Blue Corn Girl!
> Thus on the plain,
> Thus on the plain,
> Everything they revive,
> And hither return!

Second song
> Out over Great Dawn Canyon Lake
> The various fog plains be scattered
> And now from there Cloud Boys come walking
> And now from there Cloud Girls come walking.
> With little ones they come to Nambe town
> To make the children live and grow
> That, one and all, we may be happy.

Third song
> Rain waters now are falling
> Afar the thunders crash,
> Afar the lightnings gleam,
> Afar the lightnings flash
> And quickly now return.

Fourth song
> The red round fruits
> We gather in!
> The red round fruits
> We gather in!

· XXXIII ·

SONGS IN THE TURTLE DANCE AT SANTA CLARA

First song

> Long ago in the north
> Lies the road of emergence!
> Yonder our ancestors live,
> Yonder we take our being.
>
> Yet now we come southwards
> For cloud flowers blossom here
> Here the lightning flashes,
> Rain water here is falling!

Second song

> *A ha haya, ehe he,*
> *A ha haya, ehe he!*
> Fog clouds and cloud flowers
> On various mountains lie,
> Cloud flowers are blooming now
> *Te he kwa, te he kwa!*
>
> From the north the lightning
> Now makes flashes,
> The thunder rumbles now,
> Rain water now is falling!
> *A ha we ahe, aha we ahe,*
> *Aha a a a, e e he e heye!*

· XXXIV ·

SONGS OF THE RACE DANCE

The Summer People
>Old Man of the Sun
>Stand ready at dawn
>On Cactus Ridge!
>
>Old Man of the Moon!
>Stand ready at dawn
>On Cactus Ridge!
>
>Stand ready at dawn,
>Thence for San Juan!
>Stand ready at dawn,
>For Eagle-Tail-Rain-Standing Road!

The Winter People
>Little Twin White Men,
>Of Stone Man Mountain,
>Stand ready at dawn!
>
>Thence for San Juan
>Thence for Rain-Standing Road
>At San Juan!
>
>Man of the Great Night-Star
>Stand ready at dawn
>Thence for San Juan!

. XXXV ·

SONG OF AVANYU, THE STORM SERPENT

Storm Serpent Old Man
Come hither now
For here we are dancing.

Laden with rain
Now you arrive!

· XXXVI ·

SCALP DANCE SONG

Next after comes Coyote, Stretched-Out-in Dew,
Next after braves of yesterday or the day before!
To Blue Earth town of the Navahos we go
And arriving we shall kill. So that is why
Coyote, Stretched-Out-in Dew, sits straight and ready.
Wi-ya-he-na, a-nde-a-a. The next scalp!

Navajo youths! your fault alone it is
That now you die fallen along your house.
Your fault alone it is that now you die
Fallen along your house with earth-streaked thighs,
That now your mouths are stopped and streaked with
    earth.
Ho-o-wi-na,a-ye-a-a. The next scalp!

Part III

MAGIC SONGS AND PRAYERS

· XXXVII ·

THAT BUFFALO MAY COME

From far away frozen Buffalo Country
Hither now they come with their little ones,
Rapidly now they walk, rapidly they walk.
Even now they reach the Red Bird Cap.

Oh Buffalo Old Man! Oh Buffalo Old Woman!
Come hither rapidly with your little ones.
To Y'o pha k'ewe come with your little ones.

They bring to us long life together
And even now they reach Tesuque!

· XXXVIII ·

SONG OF THE HUNTER'S WIFE

Now comes the deer up to our house
He brings the needed food of life,
While we give needed food to him.

Old women deer, old men deer,
We love you! So now come hither,
On the road that we have laid!
Come hither to our house where we
May love you! Eat now this little!

Deer Dance Nambe.
Courtesy Museum of New Mexico
Photo by T. Harmon Parkhurst

· XXXIX ·

WITH DANGLING HANDS

Come all game animals large,
Come all game animals small,
Hither come with dangling hands
To Nambe town! So now come all
To Nambe town with dangling hands!

· XL ·

WHEN THE DEER COME

So the deer will hear
        Our elder brother deer,
        Our elder sister deer,
        We are going to meet you,
        We are going to meet you.

They meet the deer
        Then deer will come,
        Then deer will come,
        Come on with us
        Come on with us.
        Na-e-e-e, Ya-e-e-e-na
        Na-e-e-e, ya-e-e-e-na.

When the deer dance.
        Now you follow us
        Now you follow us
        Here we are dancing
        Here we are dancing
        In this manner
        In this manner
        Yo-ha-ri-yo, yo-ha-ri-yo
        A-a-a-he-yo-o.

· XLI ·

EAGLE SONG

On Leaf-Long Mountain
Rabbit Old Woman, Old Man!
Hereabouts they walk.
They are my dear ones!
Ya'a héya, héya
E'e ni ya, ni ya hé.

· XLII ·

SPEECH FOR GOOD TRADING

Now round about I guess you are,
You enemy peoples of strange speech
Such as you O Utes, such as you, O Kiowas,
Such as you O Comanches, such as you O Cheyennes,
Such as you O Pawnees, where you are,
Such as you, O warring peoples all!

So now from here I think of you,
From here I call aloud your names,
With money to trade for your good work
Of aching backs and sweating brows.
And when your village we have reached,
And you have something not for sale,
Easily may it come into our hands!

That is what we wish and therefore
I speak now that this to us may happen!

Woman grinding corn.

· XLIII ·

WHEN THE FIRST FRUITS ARE TAKEN

Oh Summer Leaf! Our old man,
Now I bring you fruits
From our weary labors.
Then eat and being strong
Give food again to us!

· XLIV ·

WHEN THE CORN MOTHERS ARE FED

The Bear Priest sings and throws meal on the altar
    Now and here
    My gods I give you
    This corn meal
    And thank you.

The People join and throw meal on the altar
    Now and here,
    Our old women Gods,
    Take this!
    Long life give us
    And our children!

· XLV ·

PRAYER FOR LONG LIFE

Our old women gods, we ask you!
Our old women gods, we ask you!
Then give to us long life together,
May we live until our frosted hair
Is white; may we live till then
This life that now we know!

Our old women gods,
Come hither,
Take this!
Long life give us
And our people!

We bring you meal
For arm-leg nourishment
Then grant to us
Our span of life
And to our children also!

· XLVI ·

WHEN THE CHILD IS NAMED

*The mother and godmother on the housetop before dawn:
the godmother speaks:*

   My Sun!
   My Morning Star!
   Help this child to become a man.
   I name him
   Rain-dew Falling!
   I name him
   Star Mountain!

The mother throws a live coal: the godmother throws sacred meal.

. XLVII .

WHEN THE MAN TAKES OFFICE

The summer cacique speaks:
    Here and now my arm,
    Painted Sand-burrs Bringing,
    Of the Sun People, chosen
    Old-woman, old-man to be:
    Accept this governor's staff,
    Agree now to help it
    Protect it, obey it, love it.

The new governor replies:
    Here and now, my fathers,
    Summer priest, Winter priest,
    I hear your words and obey them.

. XLVIII .

LAST WORDS AT THE GRAVE

Eat the food that now we bring you
And remember us no more!
Give us ample food, and now
No longer we remember you!

· XLIX ·

WHEN THE SCALPS ARE FED

Down yonder at their village
The Navaho youths lie scalped,
The young men of Santa Clara
Those blue-bird skins stripped off.

· L ·

DEAD ON THE WAR PATH

This very day, a little while ago, you lived
But now you are neither man nor woman,
Breathless you are, for the Navahos killed you!
Then remember us not, for here and now
We bring you your food. Then take and keep
Your earth-walled place: once! twice!
Three times! four times! Then leave us now!

APPENDIX

Abbreviations used in referring to articles:

A.A.   American Anthropologist. References to volume number, old series (O.S.) and new series (N.S.).

A.M.N.H.   American Museum of Natural History—Memoirs (Mem.) and Anthropological Papers (Anth. Pap.) referred to by number.

B.A.E.   Bureau of American Ethnology, Annual Reports (Ann. Rep.) and Bulletins (Bull.) referred to by number.

J.A.F.   Journal of American Folk-Lore.

L.A.A.L.   Library of American Aboriginal Literature, edited by D. G. Brinton, referred to by author and separate title.

M.A.F.S.   Memoirs of the American Folk-Lore Society.

P.A.E.S.   Publications of the American Ethnological Society.

U.C.P.   University of California Publications in American Archaeology and Ethnology.

NOTES ON INTRODUCTORY ESSAY

1   Kroeber, A. L. *Handbook of the Indians of California*, B.A.E., Bull. 78, p. 511.

2   La Flesche, F. *The Osage Tribe*, Published in four parts: I, B.A.E., 36th Ann. Rep. II, B.A.E., 39th Ann. Rep. III, B.A.E., 43rd Ann. Rep. IV., B.A.E., 45th Ann. Rep. Reference in I, pp. 85-86.

3   Idem, III, p. 530.

4   Brinton, D.G. *Ancient Nahuatl Poetry*, L.A.A.L., vol. VII, p. 41.

5   Idem, pp. 45-47.

6   Rendered from the Spanish of Lafone Quevado, S. A., *El Culto de Tonapa*, Revista Museo de la Plata, III, pp. 323-379, with reference to the translations of Markham, Sir C. R., *The Incas of Peru*, London, 1910, pp. 100-101 and Means, P. A., *Ancient Civilizations of the Andes*, New York, 1931, pp. 437-438. Other Peruvian poems are admirably discussed in the last mentioned work, and their sources given.

7   Wissler, C., *The American Indian*, New York, 1917, pp. 143-144.

8   Grosse, E. *The Beginnings of Art*, New York, 1897, pp. 224.

9   A study of the musical tones of two-lipped drums has recently been published by the National Museum of Mexico: Castaneda, D. and Mendoza, V. T. *Los Teponaztles en las civilizaciones precortesianas*, Anales del Museo Nacional de Archeologia, Historia y Ethnografia, Vol. VIII, No. 1, pp. 1-80. John E. Cornyn insists that the Aztecs employed the trochaic meter; in his *Song of Quetzalcoatl* he uses Hiawatha-like versification.

10   Brinton, D. G. Op. cit., pp. 106, 121, 125.

11   Densmore, R. *Chippewa Music;* Published in two parts: I, B.A.E., Bull. 45, II, B.A.E., Bull. 53. This reference in I, p. 41.

12   Whiffen, T. *The Northwest Amazons*, p. 190.

13   Thalbitzer, W. *The Ammassalik Eskimo*, Part II, No. 3, *Language and Folklore*, Copenhagen, 1923, p. 206. This report is published in a Danish serial devoted to the scientific description of Greenland, some articles being in Danish and some in English.

14   Swanton, J. R. *Haida Songs*, P. A. E. S., III, pp. 5 and 22.

15   Thalbitzer, W. Op. cit., pp. 211-212.

16 B.A.E., 43rd Ann. Rep., pp. 341-343.
17 Densmore, F. *Teton Sioux Music;* B.A.E., Bull. 61, pp. 165-166.
18 Densmore, F. *Chippewa Music,* I, p. 127.
19 Mooney, T. *The Ghost Dance Religion and the Sioux Outbreak* of 1890, B.A.E., 15th Ann. Rep., p. 976.
20 Thalbitzer, Op. cit., pp. 260-261.
21 Russell, F. *The Pima Indians,* B.A.E., 26th Ann. Rep., p. 290.
22 Dorsey, G. A. *The Pawnee-Mythology,* Pub. 59 Carnegie Inst. of Washington, pp. 222-225.
23 Densmore, F. *Papago Music,* B.A.E., Bull. 90, p. 173.
24 Densmore, F. *Chippewa Music,* II, pp. 253-254.
25 La Flesche, F. *The Osage Tribe,* IV, pp. 544-547.
26 Idem, I, p. 211.
27 Thalbitzer, W. Op. cit., p. 241.
28 Rink, H. J. *Tales and Traditions of the Eskimo,* London, 1875, pp. 67-68. The poem is recast in the form printed above in Brinton, D. G. *American Aboriginal Poetry,* Proc. Numismatic and Antiquarian Soc. of Philadelphia, pp. 21-22. For comparison I give Rink's translation which has a prose form but with dots to indicate the omission of the meaningless refrain. With the help of these dots the verses can be reconstructed as follows:

Savdlat

> The south, the south, oh the south yonder.
> When settling on the midland coast I met Pulangitsissok
> Who had grown stout and fat from eating halibut.
> Those people from the midland coast they don't know speaking,
> Because they are ashamed of their speech.
> Stupid they are besides.
> Their speech is not alike,
> Some speak like the northern, some like the southern;
> Therefore we can't make out their talk.

Pulangitsissok

> There was a time when Savdlat wished that I should be a good
>   kayaker,
> That I could take a good load on my kayak,
> Many years ago some day he wanted me to put a heavy load on my
>   kayak
> (This happened at the time) when Savdlat had his kayak tied to
>   mine (for fear of being capsized)
> Then he could carry plenty upon his kayak.
> When I had to tow thee, and thou didst cry most pitiful,
> And thou didst grow afeared,
> And wast nearly upset,
> And hadst to keep thy hold by help of my kayak strings.

29 Thalbitzer, W. Op. cit., p. 329.
30 Idem, pp. 246-247.
31 Rink, H. J. Op. cit., p. 68. Also recast by Brinton in the article referred to in note 28.
32 Boas, F. *Ethnology of the Kwakiutl,* B.A.E., 35th Ann. Rep., pp. 1298-1299.
33 Idem, pp. 1304-1306.

34 Densmore, F. *Chippewa Music*, I, pp. 88-90.
35 Densmore, F. *Chippewa Music*, I, p. 154.
36 Brinton, D. G. *Aboriginal American Authors*, Philadelphia, 1883, p. 48.
37 P. 89.
38 Couto de Magalães—*O Selvagem*, Rio Janeiro, 1876, pp. 140-142.
39 Swanton, J. R. *Tlingit Myths and Texts*, B.A.E., Bull. 39, pp. 409-410.
40 Idem, p. 410.
41 Idem, p. 411.
42 Boas, F. Op. cit., p. 1292.
43 Thalbitzer, W. Op. cit., p. 407.
44 Densmore, F. *Papago Music*, pp. 126, 129, 130.
45 Matthews, W. *Navaho Gambling Songs*, A.A., Vol. 2, O.S., p. 15.
46 Idem, p. 9.
47 Matthews, W. *Songs of Sequence of the Navajos*. J.A.F. Vol. VII. p. 186.
48 Matthews, W. *The Mountain Chant*, B.A.E., 5th Ann. Rep. p. 393.
49 Idem, p. 459.
50 Matthews, *The Night Chant*, A.M.N.H., Mem., Vol. 6, pp. 78-79.
51 Idem, pp. 279-282.
52 Idem, p. 294. *Sialia*, I may say, is the scientific name for the genus and therefore a latin word. Matthews puts it in italics.
53 Penard, A. P. and T. E. *Popular Notions Pertaining to Primitive Stone Artifacts in Surinam*, Jour. Am. Folk Lore, Vol. 30 (1917), pp. 251-261. I make two slight changes in the texts, using "lightning eel" instead of the native term *Pulake* and "clear the way" for "move out of the way."
54 Mooney, T. Op. cit., p. 711.
55 Idem, p. 721.
56 Kroeber, A. L. Op. cit., p. 515.
57 Mooney, T. Op. cit., p. 1052, Song No. 1. The other Paiute songs given below are Nos. 5, 6, 7, 8 and 9 on pages 1054-1055.
58 Idem, p. 961 et seq. Arapaho songs Nos. 3, 8, 28, and 72 on pages 958-1011.
59 Hale, H. *The Iroquois Book of Rites*, L.A.A.L., Vol. II, p. 153. Other examples of Iroquois religious chants are found in the writings of Arthur C. Parker, etc.
60 Lehmann, W. *Eine Tolteken-Klangesang, Festschrift Eduard Seler*, Stuttgart, 1892, pp. 281-319, reviews the texts of these ancient pieces.
    In the *Popul Vuh* of the Quiché a Toltec lament is given in part, for we read: And here they started their hymn called "We See the Dawn." They sang the dirge and their hearts, their vitals, mourned its burden.

> "Alas! we have lost each other in Tollan!
> We are dispersed and our younger brothers,
> Our elder brothers, are left behind!
> Indeed we have seen the sun—
> Where are the others now that light has come."

61 For the chronological significance of these prophesies see my *Maya Dates and What they Reveal*, Brooklyn Museum, Science Bulletin, Vol. IV., No. 1, pp. 18-21.
62 Brinton, D. G. *The Annals of the Cakchiquels*, L.A.A.L., Vol. VI, p. 77.
63 Brasseur de Bourbourg, *Popul Vuh*, Paris, 1861, pp. 31-33. There is a recent Guatamalan edition by Villacorta and Rodas entitled *Popul*

Buj. Also discussed in Alexander's volume on *Latin America* in *The Mythology of All Races*, Boston, 1922. Vol. XI, pp. 159 et seq.

64 Hills, E. C. *The Quechua Drama Ollanta*. The Romanic Review V, pp. 127-176 covers the subject of the date of this work very fully.

65 Kroeber, A. L. Op. cit., p. 757.

66 Idem, p. 96, but also see his critical notes on pp. 659-660 in the same volume.

67 La Flesche, F. *The Osage Tribe*, I, p. 288. In the four great sections of La Flesche's work the idea of the proper choice to be made in a field of material advantage finds expression over and over again. For a somewhat fuller version see II, pp. 258-259.

68 Boas F. *Stylistic Aspects of Primitive Literature*. J.A.F., Vol. 38, p. 330.

69 Seler, E. *Die Religiosen Gesange der alten Mexicaner*, Gesammelte Abhandlungen, Vol. II. The Song to Xipe Totec, pp. 1071-1078, the Song of Xochipilli in my wife's recent study of *The Place of Tajin in Totonac Archaeology* in A.A., vol. XXXV, N.S., pp. 255-256.

70 There are two slightly different renderings by D. G. Brinton, the first in his *Maya Chronicles*, pp. 126-127 and the second, which is used here in his *Essays of an Americanist*, Philadelphia, 1890, p. 303.

71 Fletcher, A. C. *The Hako: A Pawnee Ceremony*, B.A.E., 22nd Ann. Rep. Pt. II, pp. 42-48 and 290-291.

72 Russell, F. Op. cit., p. 324.

73 Spinden, H. J. *Home Songs of the Tewa Indians*, The American Museum Journal, Vol. XV, pp. 73-78, contains Songs II to X, as well as XVII, XXI and XXII. In *Indian Dances of the Southwest* in the same volume, pp. 103-115 I give the first stanza from the *Turtle Dance at Nambe* (No. XX): In *The Forum* of September, 1925 the *Song of the Sky Loom*, No. XXIX in the present collection. The remaining poems have never before been put to print.

74 Stephenson, M. C., *The Zuni Indians*, B.A.E. 23rd. Ann. Rep. p. 176.

NOTES ON TEWA POEMS

In translating the Tewa language I have made use of the ordinary conventions of phonetic writing, putting down the sounds as my ear caught them. It is to be expected that inconsistences should occur owing first to the varying enunciation of different informants from the same village and secondly to the dialectic variation among the five villages of Tesuque, Nambe, San Ildefonso, Santa Clara and San Juan. The dialectic differences are partly seen in the musical pitch or accent which I have made no effort to record. Tewa has many one syllable words and these are distinguished from each other by subtle modulations of the voice: but as a rule the context shows which one of several homonyms is meant.

The Tewa language is richly vocalized, although the vowels often have nasal qualities. The nasalization when present may be soft, or it may be harsher and more ringing. These differences can be written by a small *n* or *ng* above the affected vowel. It happens that both the musical pitch and the qualities of nasalization vary somewhat among the villages of the Tewa group and the present writer makes no claim for using all the marks of a perfect record.

In general the vowels have Continental rather than English values, to wit: *a* as in *ah*, *e* as in eight, *i* as in *machine*, *o* as in *rose*, and *u* as the final sound in *who*. Also there is a common *a* umlaut (ä), as in *man*, and another (â) with a very broad sound, the *a* in *all*. Also it will be noted by those who examine the original texts that vowels are frequently doubled in Tewa with an apostrophe written between. This apostrophe indicates a closing of the glottis and the second vowel is generally much shorter than the first, like a kind of echo. Some of the consonants are found in three forms, normal, aspirated and glottally affected. For instance we find *k*, *kh*, and *k'*, the first like the English consonant, the second a *k* stop followed by a breathing and the third having a somewhat explosive sound to the common ear. Pretty clear stress accents are used in the longer Tewa words.

Now follows a brief comment on each Tewa poem under the Roman numerals which designate them. Space does not permit a full record of the native texts but typical ones are given.

I

This ki kha'a or shouting song is sung by men at work in the fields or coming home from the hunt. It refers to the annual rabbit drive and the places mentioned are favorite hunting places of the San Juan Indians corresponding to the four directions. The Road of Magic is the Road of Life. But also it runs before the cradle and beyond the grave and is travelled by the souls of the unborn and the ghosts of the dead. Along this Magic Road come the Rain Gods, passing through lakes that are gateways of the underworld.

1

Owe P'in tsä âkonu
Yonder-at   Mountain-white   Plain
He häyago he mbo'o
Long-ago-very   it was good.
O'ke 'anyu O'ke 'enu nda
San Juan   girls   San Juan boys and
Ndi arang yi nde'e
They used to walk together.
Haran Tsi p'o na k'o inge
Where Magic-road its-lying-at.

2

Owe Yo phe âkonu . . . . .
Yonder-at   Cactus-stalk Plain

3

Owe Thun'un p'i âkonu . . . . .
Yonder-at Painted-mountain Plain.

4

Näwe Wombi ri âkonu
Here-at Medicine-hill Plain
Ho'o ngi arang yi'i
Now   we   walk   together
O'ke 'anyu O'ke 'enu nda
San Juan girls   San Juan boys and
Ho'o ngi arang yi'i
Now   we   walk-together
Haran Tsi p'o na k'o inge
Where Magic-road its-lying at.

II

The Tewa Indian easily becomes homesick even when distant a few miles from his native village. This little song, which brought tears to the eyes of one of my Tewa friends when I repeated it to him on his own hearthstone, might be called Home Sweet Home. The text given below was secured at Nambe, but I have heard a close variant at San Ildefonso. It has a perfect poetic structure with what almost amounts to rhyme although this is perhaps accidental. The Tewa singer depends upon repeated phrases for the essential pattern of his verses.

> Navi owin näwä owin näwä
> Navi owin näwä ndi on sha
> O'in p'in ndo mu'ire ka nyi nanandi
> Nâ re sitä: âhiyohe'e ewä,
> Ahiyohe' ewä, ahiyohe'ewä,
> Navi owin näwä ndi on sha.

I may say that the reduction of songs to a written text is not always easy, nor can accuracy be guaranteed. Distortions of the words are often caused by the musical measures which may be rationalized by different informants in somewhat different fashion.

III

This second song of homesickness, coming from San Juan, is the complete expression of a mood. It seems that memory is kindled, bursts into flame and burns down to gray ashes in the short space of six lines.

IV

The use of affectionate diminutives such as *hâ e*, breath-little, and *pi'e*, heart-little, is characteristic of Tewa love songs. There is emotional purity without a touch of physical passion. The text, which is followed closely in the translation, makes use of a sort of color symbolism to vary the repeated phrases. The Tewa name for a love song is se kane kha'a, and this very beautiful one comes from the village of Santa Clara.

V

The note of banter in this little love song gives a picture of rustic happiness to which no amount of fine phrases could add. The Tewa men in their cornfields sing "shouting songs," such as this, which are sometimes faintly audible to the women in the village.

VI

The comparison of a maiden and a flower is perhaps as old as any form of poetic speech. Yet one may wonder whether the excessive use of "flowery speech" by the Aztecs may not have set a fashion which spread to the north.
I give the Tewa words with the stress accents:

> Sú K'wa K'e wé na póvi tshá nde
> In póvi, in póvi, ndo mú iri
> Kányi na nándi na ré si tä!
> In póvi, in póvi, ndo mú iri
> Ts'e, okí, t'agi, na póvi tshá.

VII

Thamu or Dawn was an old man of Santa Clara who died when my informant was a child. He would sing this derisive song to the girls as they ground corn and retreat when they pelted him.

U a wä nä i sen
Alas! this man
Mbi hi'i t'u
His words voice
Nda tage wage
And truth-like
Ndi hi'i an
When he talked to me.
He mbo wese
But right away
Wi hoyo sha,
You liar found
Wi hoyo sha!
You liar found!

VIII

When the wrong man comes forward and the right one hangs back, comparisons are in order. This is a relatively modern song from Nambe and lacks the essential brevity—and clarity—of the accepted classics.

IX

The device of the colloquy is fairly common in Tewa poetry as it is in that of ancient Mexico, without, of course, any interpolation of the speaker's name. The girl in this case was nicknamed Little Blue because the door frame of her house was painted that color. Her dismissal of the errant but repentant swain ends with the phrase "it was under guns that you dared to pay", which means something done at a foolish risk.

X

Perhaps the lady doth protest too much—but at least she achieves a precise expression of bitterness.

XI

The story behind this colloquy is that of an Indian youth of San Juan who married a "Mexican" woman and went to live in Truchas. Again the flower motive is used and by comparing this piece with VI and IX it is at once apparent that here is a definite literary tradition.

XII

Two girls express their opinion of a third more fortunate one—and it does not matter whether the aspersion was just or not.

XIII

Here is a brave pretense on both sides and might be called a teasing song of parting:

T'owepiye poge we nga he'i nä
Ngo we'i nga kh a'a tu ni
Ito ki hä nyu mbai ye kin on sha
An ki rang ndi yo'an.

XIV

This khe mä'i kha'a—ready-to-go song is not particularly war-like but
the Tewa seem never to have been a warlike people. The Navaho were, of
course, the common scourge of all the sedentary tribes. I secured two variant
texts, the shorter one running:

>Na'imbi kwiyo'in unda ihä
>Nâ' in se nän wigi hä pi
>Wâ save owinge piye i khe mä

XV

This song has been transcribed by Alice Corbin Henderson in her *Red Earth*.
The Tewa text runs about as follows:

>Nä t'o me impi yere
>Nä so'okuwa ko
>Nä so'okuwa ko
>Yare Khun tsâ wai'i
>Yagi wani na kha tu'un
>Ha we rana na' a se.

For each verse the Corn Maiden of another quarter is named according
to the accepted symbolism of colors.

XVI

This is a corn grinding song. I think the blue flowers which grow around
the sacred lake of Nambe on Lake Peak are meant. The significant words are:

>Povi tsâ wä t'u
>Opa keri tu na sa
>Tsi ko wa tin ki na sa

Corn grinding songs are of two kinds. The Ta kha's are sung by the
girls themselves keeping time to the strokes of the hand stones. The other
kind called Nu ta kha's, night grinding songs, are sung by the men.

XVII

Another corn-grinding song.

XVIII

This was described as War Captain's Song, this officer having charge of
the work outside the town.

XIX

The 'e kha'a, meaning child song is, of course, our lullaby. The verses vary
only in accordance with the circuit of the four directions. The text for the
last verse is:

>Tampiye okhuwa povi napovisa
>*In the east cloud flower the blossom stands*
>Nda ng'u tsiguweno ko'in mu we'a
>*And then the lightning begins to flash*
>Nda ng'u kwan ta'a ita'a
>*And then the thunder it thunders*
>Nda ng'u kwa'a pose yemu
>*And then the fine rain falls*
>A' a' a ha.

XX

No comment is called for.

XXI

Here the little boy born in the spring, as we may know from his springtime name Primrose, is old enough to have experienced the discipline of the Cannibal Giants. These terrifying masked creatures come to the village with whips and children who have been disobedient do not enjoy their performances.

XXII

Here the little girl has an autumnal name. The sleepy little birds, which are caught on the mountain and kept as pets, are supposed to have a sympathetic influence on the child.

XXIII

This song is sung by children at play.

> Sagi wo nging povi sa,
> Mbe ndu nde'e nging povi sa,
> P'o pe'e nging povi sa,
> I 'ang ho' nging povi sa.

XXIV

The K'osa or Delight Makers belong to three orders, the Kwirana K'osa, the Tewa K'osa and the Tema K'osa. This initiation chant of the Kwirana K'osa expresses the high spiritual purpose of these sacred clowns. It seems that the institution is distributed among all the village Indians of the Southwest. Mrs. Matilda Cox Stephenson gives ceremonial material on the Kwirana organization at Sia and I quote for comparison part of a song secured by her:

> White floating clouds, clouds like plains,
> Sun, Moon, Puma, Bear, Badger, Wolf
> Eagle, Shrew, Elder War Hero, Younger War Hero,
> Warrior of the North, Warrior of the West,
> Warrior of the South, Warrior of the East,
> Warrior of the Above, Warrior of the Below,
> Medicine Water Bowl, Cloud Bowl, Ceremonial Water Bowl,
> I make a road of meal, the ancient road, the ancient road.

At the Hopi villages the order is called Pai-a kya-muh according to Fewkes (A Journal of American Ethnology II pp. 10—11), a name which seems to have been derived from Than phaiya tchamu of the Tewa text. Of course Hano on the First Mesa is really a Tewa village.

> Näwe ho'o we ma'a na imbi sendo'in
> *Here-at now we bring you Oh our old men*
> Than phaiya tshama Okhuwa tsâ wä'in
> *Sun-fire- deity Cloud person blue*
> Than phaiya tshama Okhuwa tse'nyin
> *Sun-fire- deity Cloud person yellow.*
> Than phaiya tshama Okhuwa p'i'in
> *Sun-fire- deity Cloud person red*
> Than phaiya tshama Okhuwa tsä'in
> *Sun- fire- Cloud person white*

Than phaiya tshama Okhuwa nu khu win
Sun-fire deity Cloud person dark
Than phaiya tshama Okhuwa tsä neg'in
Sun-fire-deity Cloud person all colors
Nä we we ma'a ho'o ovi pi tuwä phe
Here at we bring you now your heart-hunt-stick
O mi gi'in ovi p'o sa k'u wiri
We make it for you tobacco to smoke
O mi gi'in ovi khu khi ko puri
We make it for you cornmeal to eat
Hâ wo'a omi gi'in ovi
Little bit for all we make it for you
Thamu khe nyi ye'gi'in p'in piye p'in k'eri
At dawn ready to walk be northward mountain top
Tso mpi ye hwage yoge p'in k'eri
Westward lakewards great mountain top
O ko mpiye tshu sogi p'in k'eri
Southward where the Shu sit mountain top
Than piye thamu yogi p'in k'eri
Eastward dawn-great mountain top
Opa makori p'in k'eri
Universe-sky mountain top
Nan soge nuge p'in k'eri
Earth-sit-under-at mountain top
Okhuwa povi phi si ni nge p'i
Cloud flowers that are not barren
Oving okhuwa povi pi ye iwe
You-them cloud flowers when you bring there-at
We to p'in piye p'in k'eri
Far off northward mountain top
Oving okhuwa povi soge iwe
You-them cloud flowers set there-at
Tsom piye p'i k'eri
Westward mountain top
Oving okhuwa povi soge iwe
You-them cloud flowers set there-at
Akom piye p'i k'eri
Southward mountain top
Oving okhuwa povi soge iwe
You-them cloud flowers set there-at
Than piye p'in k'eri
Eastward mountain top
Oving okhuwa povi soge iwe
You-them cloud flowers set there-at
Opa makori p'in k'eri
Universe-sky mountain top
Oving okhuwa povi soge iwe
You-them cloud flowers set there-at
Nan soge nuge p'in k'eri
Earth-sitting-below mountain top
Oving okhuwa povi soge iwe
You-them cloud flowers set there-at

P'in pinu oving sokhuwa pa'are k'u'u iwe
Mountain middle you-them fogs first lay there-at
Iwe ha ndi re Ok'e owinge piye
There-at that is why San Juan town towards
Oving tha mu khe ma iwe
You-them at dawn ready bring there-at
Umbi tsigu wänu kwa ta kwa p'o wogi
Your lightning thunder rain together
Khi ye nava k'u p'in nge heri
Transform farms lying-in-middle and
Ovi thamu khe kâng ndiwe
You dawn ready have come there-at
He ndi ri ako na k'o igi heri
That is why plain where-it is lying and
Ha ndi ri ako p'in wo'o pa k'wone
That is why plains-mountains revived lie
Ha ndi ri ho'o umbi t'a p'o kwin
That is why now your drying lakes
Un k'wo ni nge ho'o
Your where they are lying now
Oving wo'a pa k'wo ne iwe
You-them revived lie there-at
Tsing we nu hä pang ri mbo'e
Tame animals one-and-all children
T'ä t'o wa 'e gin sigi muni
All little people to be loved by the gods
We nge naimbi kwiyo
Till where our Great Mother's
Ndi hâ sa k'a 'a po wa in ge heri
Her breath-sound reaches even-till there
Yuta, Savi, Wa savi, Kai wa,
Utes, Apaches, Navajo, Kiowa
Komantsi, Tsaiyena iwe ri mbo'o
Comanche, Cheyenne there-at all
K'wä k'u towa ndi mu in iwe ri mbo'o
Mexican people they are the ones there-at all
Americano t'owa ndi mu'in
American people they are the ones
We nge naimbe kwi yo'un
Till there our Great Mother's
Ndi hâ sa k'a'a powa mge heri
Her breath-sound reaches even-till there
Ho'o ri sigi mu ni ndi seka ni
Now they loved by the gods, they by each other
Ina hai ndi ri ngi piva
So that is why we expect
Ngi hu nä säta t'o wa k'eri
We will eat here we-mortals-on-earth
Nyä ra'i pá yo, nyä ra'i i phoye khu tha
Good summer good harvest night-day
Ha'a ming pho ye tha-khu nding k'u we
The-same-kind harvest day-night, may they place.

XXV

In this Initiation Song of the Tewa K'osa the novitiate jests at Kâkanyu Sendo and Uhu Sendo, two of the Cloud People who wear masks with large, ring-shaped eyes. When the K'osa exclaims that the round eyes are being carried off in the water the implication is that the rain gods themselves are being swept away. When pursued by the seemingly angry gods he makes quick disclaimer. He declares that he meant only the little cakes strung on a string which symbolize these round eyes.

> To mba mbuge i'kwâ na
> 'I hä ha enyu ip'o k'u re
> Kâ kanyu sendo tsi ts'e thagi 'o p'o ho
> To mba mbuge i'kwâ na
> 'I hä ha enyu i p'o k'u re
> Uhu sendo tsi ts'e thagi 'op'o ho
> Yo navi sendo! yo navi sendo!
> Ka paweno ndo toma.

XXVI

This is described as a very sad pi nan kha'a or magic song of the Tewa K'osa which all the Indians know but are afraid to sing. It means the K'osa are going in under a sacred lake to the place where the rains and the lightnings are made, all lakes being regarded as entrances to the underworld. This song is sung on the shore of a certain lake in the Santa Fé mountains especially sacred to Nambe.

XXVII

This passage is taken from a long myth of Nambe. It illustrated several ceremonial usages of the K'osa: one is that they sometimes say the opposite of what they mean such as designating one direction and performing in another. The "lakes" where the gods dwell may be only green spots. But the path of the rainbow upon which they travel is thrown from one such station to the next.

XXVIII

This song is from the Flood Myth and is sung by Urn-tu-sendo, Walking Stick Old man, who may be described as the Tewa Adam. When the flood comes his daughters, the Blue Corn Girls are floated upward to the sky in a basket and after adventures in the Sky World are lowered again to earth by the Spider Woman.

XXIX

The sky loom I have already explained in the general introductory essay as referring to the small desert rains which resemble a loom hung from the sky. There are indications that this idea was applied elsewhere in the Southwest and of course the symbolical decoration on the white cotton mantle, once the regular dress but now put to ceremonial uses, is in accordance with this chant or prayer for well-being.

XXX

The Sang khiu kwiyo or Corn Silk Women of San Juan are probably more or less the same as the Pun kha kwiyo of Nambe and the Nan hwa kwiyo Tesuque. They are a society who play a special role in certain very sacred dances connected with fertility. They appear in the Kwiyo or Woman's Dance. In this chant there are several examples of what my informants call "high words" such as wowa tsi, literally "life eye" but really "hale old age," 'e t'owa sowe, literally "children people grow up" but with the normal meaning of "rear many children". Si ge muni means "under the loving protection of the gods".

P'in piye P'o kwinge'in
Northward Lake ones
Säng khiung kwiyo i mu 'in
Corn-silk Old Women ye are the ones
Nä we ho ipowa
Here-at now ye have come
Wowatsi ho'e k'un ku'u
Long-life at once trade-lay
'E gin sigi muni
Children they to be loved of the gods
Ma'imbe'e ndivi'e t'owa sowe
Our children their children people grow up
O'ke 'anyu nda wowa tsi
San Juan girls they long-life.
Ho'e nu wä nä we ho
At once we seek here-at now
Säng khiung kwiyo nda
Corn silk Old women say
Tung wage ho ivi an
Words like now we did
Wowatsi ho ngin ka'a po
Life-long now we ask
Ho ngin sigi muni
Now we to be loved
I vi 'e t'owa sowe
We children people grow up
Nyä ra'ing hä ndi mä ni
Good fate to us give.

XXXI

This is a kwa pinan kha'a or Rain-Magic song, from the Than khohe share or Sun-Hummingbird Dance of San Juan. The humming bird is a symbol of the flowering season and this magic song is accompanied by the sprinkling of water with feather aspergils. Here the action of the ceremony is designed to suggest similar action by the gods.

O'ke owinge nä we ho ngi win
Na'imbi Khun 'anyu, Khun 'enu,
Khun yiya'in, Khun ta'in
Nä ho ngi ekang kwa p'o se
Tchänu nde täme piye
P'in piye, Tsân piye, Akon piye, Than piye,
Opa makori, Nan suge u'unge,
Ha ndiri näwe ring kwa p'o se yemu ire
O'ke owinge maimbe Khun 'anyu.
Ndi oye phoge p'o kwire
Tata 'anyu nding p'ose tchänu
Iwe ire häwi tä ki näri
Nan otchu kwi mbi tu' k'igi na sa'in
Naimbe tu hân na mui we ho nâ pa'in
Na'in wi kho khun ami rin ho na'in eko'in

The words for the six directions are interestingly different. Below is Nan suge u'unge, earth drinking below. The Underworld is personified as male, as is the Sky, while the Earth itself is female. Here the earth is Nan otchu kwiyo, Earth-fresh-green-woman.

XXXII

The Oku share or Turtle Dance is a winter ceremony having to do with fertility, the Ok huwa or Cloud People who come to this ceremony bring with them the seeds of various plants and they are also asked to ensure that children will be plentiful: the dance is there also called 'E pinan share. Children's Magic Dance. I give four songs from the sets used at Nambe which refer to the revival of the vernal season and the rains which will bring the harvest to maturity.

XXXIII

Two songs from the Turtle Dance at Santa Clara give further indication of the nature of the magical prayers, made in the form of songs, to perfect the lot of human beings. The second song, omitting meaningless refrains, has the following words:

> So'okuwa okhuwa povi
> *Fog clouds, cloud flowers*
> Tä mä p'in nä
> *Various mountains on*
> Okhuwa povi sa ho'o
> *Cloud flowers put forth now*
> P'in phâ geri tsigu wänu
> *From the north lightning*
> Ho'o re mu wa'a
> *Now it flashes*
> Kwâ t'an ho'o re ta'a
> *Thunder now rumbles*
> Kwâ p'o ho'o re yemu.
> *Rain water now is falling.*

XXXIV

The Tewa villages are all divided into two groups of clans, one commonly known as the Summer People and the other as the Winter People. The Race Dance seems to be a special magical effort to relieve the Sun in its travels, especially while the Sun seems tired at the solstices. Some idea of the astronomical significance appears in the words. The Great-Star of the Dark Night Man appears to be Jupiter.

Summer People's Song

> Than sendo i thamu khe winu Yophe k'ewe
> *Sun Old Man he at dawn ready must stand Cactus Stalk Ridge on.*
> P'o sendo wa'a i thamu khe winu Yophe k'ewe
> *Moon Old Man also he at dawn ready must stand, Cactus Stalk Ridge on*
> Mba i thamu khe winu iwe ra han O'ke owinge
> *And he at dawn ready must stand thence going San Juan toward*
> I thamu khe ho'o tse hwä kwa wi p'o.
> *He at dawn ready now Eagle Tail Rain Standing Road.*

Winter People's Song

Towa'e tsä'i'i seng K'u seng p'i neri
Little People White Men Stone-Man-Mountain from
Mbi thamu khe winu O'ke owinge piye
You two at dawn ready must stand San Juan town towards
Kwa wi p'o ge O'ke owinge piye
Rain Standing Road at San Juan town towards
Agoyo nu khu seng i thamu khe winu
Great-Star-Dark-Night Man at dawn ready must stand
O'ke owinge piye.
San Juan town towards.

XXXV

Avanyu or P'o anyu is pictured as a horned serpent often with clouds attached to his body and a tongue of barbed lightning. He is a dreaded god of storms, sometimes glimpsed in dark swirling clouds. Once this water monster threatened to flood the world but he was turned from this evil intention by twin war gods, called Towa'e or Little People, who slew him with their arrows and left his body lying as the rocky barriers of Nambe falls. The diminished flood still pours out of his great mouth and offerings are made to appease him if the stream rises suddenly. In another conception he resides in sacred lakes and moves in storm clouds. Almost certainly the various plumed and horned serpents of the Southwest are a far-off echo of the feathered serpent of the Mayas and Mexicans.

As a rule the name Avanyu is anathema. This short religious song in which he is appealed to comes from the Than kwa share, or Sun-Rain Dance, of Nambe held just before the sun reaches his northern Sun House at the summer solstice. At San Juan foot races are held in connection with the same event.

Avanyu Sendo
Storm Serpent Old Man
Ho'o kä'ä
Now come hither
Mbe nä we ivi yare nde'e
For here we are dancing
Umbi kwâ wogi
Your rain-with
Näwe u powa
Here you arrive!

XXXVI

The Scalp Dance was especially developed at Santa Clara or perhaps a memory of the ceremony has survived there in more perfect state than elsewhere. It seems that Coyote gets his ceremonial name Stretched-Out in-Dew as a devourer of slain warriors. The text of the second part of this song is as follows:

Wasävi 'e nu wi mbo'o
Navajo youths but yourselves
Hä nyi ipi nda'a ri
That way you have to blame
Umbi te'e hwa wige'e
Your house along the end of

Itshu hwa k'o ho'o
You die stretched-out lying now
Wembo'o ipi na'a ri
But yourselves you have to blame
Pu nan kang ngi wagi
Thighs earth-covered-and-streaked
Itshu hwa k'o ho'o
You die stretched-out lying now
Umbi te'e hwa wige'e
Your house along the end of
So nan kang ngi wagi.
Mouth earth-covered and streaked!

XXXVII

This piece is entitled Ko'on pinan kha'a ndi a iri—Buffalo Magic Song, Making Come. It is an example of the coercive use of song. The first place name Ko'on tsi pogi is a name for part of the Great Plains, Phi yo pi wi i is a pass near the head of the Pecos River and Yo pha k'ewe is an old town belonging to Tesuque.

Kaya 'a wimba'a Ko'on tsi pogi
Far over yonder Buffalo-Ice-Water-at
Nä piye ho'o ve mä ä imbi 'e wogi
Hither now they-them bringing their children together
A 'nyugi ho'o vi ä â tuye
Quickly now they-with-them walk quickly
Heri ho'o ndi powa Phiyo pin wi'i.
And now they arrive Red Bird Gap
Ko'on sendo, Ko'on kwiyo
Buffalo Old Man, Buffalo Old Woman
A'n yuge ho'o vi kä'ä ve umbi'e wogi
Quickly now ye-with-them come your children together
Nä piye Yo'pha k'ewe owingi umbi 'e wogi
Hither Cactus-row-ridge town-at your children together

Ndin k'on wowatsi wogi
They-to-us bring life together
Nä we ho'o in powa Te tsuge owinge.
Here-at now they arrive Tesuque town-at.

XXXVIII

While her husband is hunting the deer, the woman tries her magic. She lays a cotton thread as a road leading into her house and sits in a corner and sings this magical song.

XXXIX

To come with dangling hands is to come head down over the hunter's shoulder.

XL

In the Deer Dance at Nambe, as at other pueblos of the Rio Grand, the dancers costumed to represent deer, elk, antelope, mountain sheep and mountain goats, make a dramatic entrance into the dance plaza. This is the song of welcome made by the chorus.

XLI

This is a Tesuque song used in the Eagle Dance.

XLII

When the Tewa made dangerous trips to trade with the nomadic Indians of the plains they were under the charge of their war captain. Each night of the journey one member of the party spoke this speech from a hill top, to bring good luck to the venture.

XLIII

I have taken some liberties in the arrangement of this prayer and therefore give the original text with interlinear translation. Some of the "high words" have already been discussed.

Näwe ma'a na'imbi sendo
Here-at I bring to you our old man
Payoka umbi kho khun ame
Summer Leaf your arm-leg-aid
Ri na'imbi yu si po
And our tiredness -sweat
Män k'o eri mba yeki mbo'a
You eat! and much being
Ko'gi ndi pä hu wi.
Food to us keep on giving

XLIV

The Corn Mothers are represented by little idols made from ears of corn.

XLV

Although prayers vary somewhat, these are several well-defined patterns.

XLVI

A child may be given several names.

XLVII

It is a developed idea among the Tewa that one in authority needs the qualities of both sexes.

XLVIII

There is really no tabu among the Tewa against speaking the names of the dead but apparently they believe that the spirits of the dead should leave the homes of the living.

XLIX

This is a part of the Scalp Ceremony of Santa Clara.

XL

Whenever possible a secret grave is made for the warrior who dies in battle.